THE SPY'S GUIDE: OFFICE ESPIONAGE

THE
SPY'S GUIDE:
OFFICE ESPIONAGE

HOW TO BUG A MEETING, BOOBY-TRAP YOUR BRIEFCASE, INFILTRATE THE COMPETITION, AND MORE

by H. Keith Melton and Craig Piligian
with Duane Swierczynski

QUIRK BOOKS
PHILADELPHIA

Library of Congress Cataloging in Publication Number: 2003090706

ISBN 1-931686-60-2

Printed in the United States

Typeset in Digital and Franklin Gothic

Designed by Susan Van Horn
Illustrations by Stuart Holmes

Distributed in North America by Chronicle Books
85 Second Street
San Francisco, CA 94105

10 9 8 7 6 5 4 3 2

Quirk Books
215 Church Street
Philadelphia, PA 19106
www.quirkbooks.com

CONTENTS

Foreword   xi

Introduction   1

SECTION A: UNCOVERING INFORMATION IN YOUR OFFICE

A1. Unlocking Offices and File Cabinets   6

A2. Copying Restricted Documents   9

A3. Discovering Computer Passwords   13

A4. Accessing Your Co-workers' Mail   18

A5. Reconstructing Shredded Documents   19

A6. Uncovering Company Secrets   22

A7. Monitoring Your Co-workers' Hours   25

A8. Covertly Recording Meetings You Attend   27

A9. Covertly Recording Meetings You Cannot Attend   29

A10. Shadowing Your Co-workers   32

SECTION B: SECURING YOUR WORKSPACE

B1. Booby-Trapping Your Briefcase   36

B2. Securing Your Trash   39

B3. Protecting Your Mail   42

B4. Protecting Your Internet and E-Mail Activity   44

B5. Safeguarding Your Computer   46

B6. Booby-Trapping Sensitive Documents   48

B7. Securing Your Hotel Room   50

B8. Hiding Sensitive Papers While Traveling   54

B9. Safeguarding a Meeting   56

B10. Debugging a Meeting Room   59

B11. Detecting a Phone Tap 62

B12. Concealing Objects in a Water Bottle 64

B13. Encrypting Your Address Book 68

SECTION C: GATHERING COMPETITIVE INTELLIGENCE

C1. Gaining Secrets from the Competition 72

C2. Creating a New Identity 75

C3. Disguising Your Appearance 78

C4. Sneaking into a Competitor's Annual Meeting 83

C5. Gathering Competitive Intelligence at Conventions 85

C6. Prying Trade Secrets out of Competitors 88

C7. Bugging a Trade-Show Event 93

C8. Searching a Competitor's Home, Office, or Hotel Room 96

C9. Reading a Competitor's Laptop 99

C10. Using Your Cell Phone as a Negotiation Tool 101

SECTION D: TRANSMITTING SENSITIVE INFORMATION

D1. Making Untraceable Phone Calls 104

D2. Sending Anonymous E-Mails 106

D3. Sending Anonymous Faxes 109

D4. Protecting Your Conversations 111

D5. Embedding Secret Messages in Computer Files 114

D6. Communicating Secretly with Co-workers 118

D7. Communicating with Invisible Inks 121

SECTION E: NEUTRALIZING OFFICE EMERGENCIES

E1. Passing the Company Drug Test   126

E2. Constructing a Phone Alibi Tape   128

E3. Calling in Sick   130

E4. Appearing Injured   132

E5. Leaving the Office Undetected   135

E6. Surviving Office Imprisonment   137

E7. Transforming a Briefcase into a Bulletproof Shield   142

E8. Dealing with Letter and Package Bombs   144

E9. Escaping from a High-Rise Building   147

APPENDICES

A. Padding Your Expense Report   152

B. Operating in "Office Stealth Mode"   157

C. Securing Your Company   159

D. The Moscow Rules   161

E. Spy Products and Services   163

ACKNOWLEDGMENTS   166

ABOUT THE AUTHORS   167

by Oleg Kalugin, retired KGB Major General

Two things about this book greatly impress me.

First, I am impressed that this book even exists. When I was involved in the espionage business during my three decades in the KGB, my associates and I spent a great deal of time and effort trying to learn the secrets of our intelligence counterparts in America. We wanted to know how they were able to intercept particular messages, solicit certain kinds of information, and develop particular types of spying devices. Now, some 20 years later, I am paging through this manuscript and staring back at me are the very secrets we wanted to learn during the Cold War. Seeing these secrets in print for the first time—for less than $20—almost makes me laugh. Almost.

Unless you used to work for me, or worked for my counterparts in the Mossad (the Israeli intelligence service) or MI6 (the UK intelligence service), you won't quite appreciate how shocking some of these secrets still are—or, more to the point, that they're now available to the general public.

Secondly, I am impressed that the authors have been so methodical and effective in chronicling the fundamental secrets of our craft. I first met one of the authors, Keith Melton, nine years ago in Moscow. His avowed specialty was the technology of espionage; my expertise was more in the human side of tradecraft—recruitment, disinformation, and the like. Our first encounter was extremely productive; I believe I learned as much from him as he did from me. Straight away, I was impressed with Keith's scholarly attitude. He is no mere spy hobbyist or weekend dabbler; Keith digs deep and pursues information with a single-minded determination. I admire his eagerness, his determination, and his body of knowledge about the intelligence business.

Keith has been particularly fearless when it comes to searching out and obtaining gadgets and spy equipment throughout the Middle East, Germany, and Poland. I have been worried for Keith's physical safety over the years, but his genuine interest in recording the technical history of espionage has no doubt kept him out of trouble. He has taken some risks, but so far, so good.

I hope that you will find Keith and Craig's hard work—and the fundamentals secrets of the espionage craft—as impressive and interesting as I do. If only I had been able to get my hands on a copy of this book 20 or 30 years ago.

We might all be living in a different world.

Major General Oleg Kalugin worked 32 years for the KGB and recruited his first American spy in 1958. His career in espionage is detailed in his memoir, The First Directorate. *He also collaborated with former CIA director William Colby to help produce Activision's computer game "SpyCraft: The Great Game." General Kalugin is now a professor at the Center for Counterintelligence and Security Studies in Washington, D.C.*

It was a gorgeous sunny afternoon in Hollywood, but the temperature inside the conference room was icy cold. The executives gathered around the table didn't want to be there—but their small independent movie studio was on the verge of bankruptcy, and it was time to cut their losses.

The target buyer was easy prey. He was a young newcomer to the Southern California scene, and had no idea that the studio was desperate to sell. In fact, the whole negotiation seemed stacked in the studio's favor: They knew the newcomer had financing—lots of financing—lined up and they were determined to squeeze every last dollar out of him.

But after just twenty minutes of formalities and small talk, the newcomer surprised everyone by cutting to the chase. "I've got a plane to catch," he said. "So instead of you pretending that you don't want to sell your studio, and me pretending that I don't want to buy it, let's save ourselves some time. I'm going to visit your men's room. While I'm gone I want you to decide the lowest price you need to make this deal happen. And when I come back, we'll see if we can make it work."

As the newcomer made a beeline for the men's room, the executives were already huddling with their advisers. When he returned a few minutes later, the newcomer made an offer that was preposterously low—it was just barely more than the studio needed to pay off its debts. Yet the stunned executives had no choice but to make the deal—and that film studio has since gone on to become one of the most profitable ventures in the industry.

So how did the newcomer pull it off? You can learn the trick yourself on page 101; it's just one of many spy-based skills that are often used, but seldom acknowledged, in the business world. Over the course of this book, you'll also learn how to uncover office secrets, send anonymous e-mails, discover your boss's computer password, find out when your co-workers are really leaving the office at night, and even learn how to turn your briefcase into a bulletproof shield.

Most of these skills originated in the world's intelligence services. We began chronicling these tricks of the trade decades ago when we visited the spy capitals of Europe and the Middle East. Our research into the classic skills of espionage accelerated in the 1990s following the collapse of communism; suddenly, we had access to locations that had once been closed.

We've benefited from suggestions by a number of retired intelligence officers, from the legendary Markus Wolf (head of East Germany's external intelligence service, the HVA) to the technical experts of the Mossad (Israeli intelligence service) and the CIA's retired "Master and Mistress of Disguise," Tony and Jonna Mendez.

We soon learned that the technical training received by most spies is surprisingly similar; the same techniques used to open locks, search rooms, conduct surveillance, and safeguard secrets are employed by intelligence officers around the world. Without the help and suggestions of these professionals who shared their craft with us, this book would not have been possible.

Over the course of our research and extensive travel, our friends and family back home would often ask: What do real spies look like? They imagined James Bond, Austin Powers, or the infamous Mata Hari. The truth is, all they needed to do was look around their offices. Spying isn't a relic of the Cold War or something that only happens in novels and in movies; it is a part of everyday business life.

Collecting competitive intelligence (gathering information about your business competitors) and safeguarding our own secrets is an ongoing struggle. Businesspeople who believe they are immune from attack are an easy target. Conversely, businesspeople who think they don't need the very best information—the secret stuff—about their competitors are missing an enormous opportunity for success.

In short, a real business spy can look like anybody. Like you, for instance.

—H. Keith Melton and Craig Piligian

SECTION A
UNCOVERING INFORMATION IN YOUR OFFICE

A I

UNLOCKING OFFICES AND FILE CABINETS

In the movies, trenchcoat-wearing spies pick locked drawers and doors in seconds. That's ridiculous. In reality, picking a lock can require hours of finger-numbing work, and there's no guarantee of success. A much better solution is to create a duplicate key. Since asking to borrow the original key from your boss might make him or her a tad suspicious, you should wait until you have access to the key and then make a quick impression, which can be used to make a duplicate key.

① **Empty a small, flat metal box with either a hinged or sliding lid.** A breath-mint box will work fine; just make sure the box is longer and wider than the target key.

② **Fill the box with modeling clay.** Some use soap to make a key impression, but modeling clay is preferable since it doesn't shrink and retains almost all of the detail of the original key. Smooth the clay so it is completely flat and level.

3 **Sprinkle a thin layer of talcum powder over the surface of the clay.** This will prevent clay from sticking to the key.

4 **Obtain the key.** This is probably not as tough as you think. People are creatures of habit, and your boss probably leaves his or her keys in the same place every day. Try their purse or briefcase when they've left them unattended. Maybe there's a copy of the key you want in their assistant's desk. (Even assistants need to eat lunch.) Maybe you can nab it while the boss is in the fitness room and his or her locker is open. All you need are a few moments alone with the key.

5 **Press the key firmly into the clay.** You will need to make two impressions—one of each side—to ensure that the measurements can be taken accurately. Make a mental note of the name of the key manufacturer or scratch it into the clay beside the imprint.

(6) **Wipe the key clean before returning it.** A cooperative locksmith can use the impression to produce a key by the same manufacturer within minutes—and finding a cooperative locksmith is easier than you'd think. People often lose keys, and locksmiths are familiar with strange requests. (One locksmith we know once had to free a woman from a chastity belt after her husband lost the key.) Claiming that you made the impression as a safeguard in case the original was lost will sound believable, especially if you are groomed and well dressed. An attractive young woman will be even more successful, especially if she can produce tears to convince the locksmith of the trouble she'll be in if she comes home without the key.

EXPERT TIP: No time to make an impression? In a pinch, lay the target key on a photocopier and copy both sides. It helps to lay a small millimeter-scale ruler parallel to the key when making the copy. A skilled locksmith can work from a paper copy, so long as the copy was not reduced or enlarged from the original. Though this is more difficult and time consuming, it can be done.

A2

COPYING RESTRICTED DOCUMENTS

Once you have a key to a target office or file cabinet, you can't just waltz on in. Wait for everyone to leave for the day, then enter the office. When you find the desired documents, you'll need to make a copy—without using the copy machine. Some companies use camera surveillance in the copy room and/or check the number of copies produced each day; an extra 300 copies made overnight may set off alarm bells. And every photocopier leaves a telltale "fingerprint"—scratches and imperfections in the glass that can be used to trace the copied document back to a specific copy machine. It is best to photograph the document where you find it.

(1) **Select the right camera.** Many different types of cameras can be used to photograph documents, but for clandestine work, a 35 mm SLR (single lens reflex), either digital or film, is ideal. The advantage of an SLR camera is that the image in the viewfinder is the exact image that will appear in the picture. If the target office must be searched in total darkness (using night-vision glasses or a small flashlight), select a recent-model 35 mm camera loaded with high-speed infrared film. Cover the face of the flash unit (be careful not to cover the small red infrared preflash) with a Wratten Gelatin filter. This will allow you use of the flash in darkness.

EXPERT TIP: High-quality digital cameras allow you to review your work after each shot to confirm quality. Additionally, digital cameras can produce exceptional results in low and varying light situations. (See Appendix E for recommended brands.) Some high-end cameras are so exceptionally sensitive that it is possible to photograph documents using only the light of a single birthday candle or a dimmed flashlight.

(2) **Prepare the camera in advance.** The best camera in the world is useless if you forget the film or the batteries, or if you're constantly referring to the instruction manual.

(3) **Practice, practice, practice.** Develop a consistent technique for copying documents in an environment where lighting conditions are similar to those of the target location. Be sure you are producing images of sufficient quality.

(4) **Strip all packaging from the film cassettes.** Never take any waste material into the target office that can be discarded beforehand. Even the most lax employee may become suspicious if he or she arrives at work and finds the waste receptacles overflowing with discarded film wrappers.

(5) **Photograph the most important documents first.** You never know if you'll be interrupted or if you'll need to limit your operational time.

(6) **Use a camera stand.** This arrangement is especially helpful if you're photographing a large number of documents. Either bring a collapsible stand with you, or rig one on the spot (see illustration).

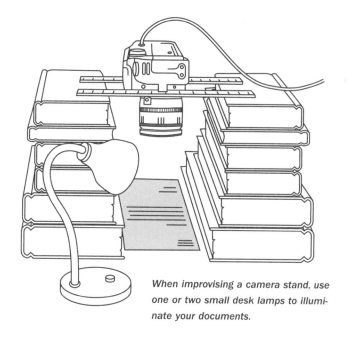

When improvising a camera stand, use one or two small desk lamps to illuminate your documents.

(7) **Upon completion, inventory and repack all photographic equipment.** Verify that all film cassettes and digital media are accounted for. Return all copied materials to their original locations. Close all file cabinets and drawers. If you had to unlock them, make sure they're locked.

(8) **Get the hell out of there.**

SPIES AT WORK

The most damaging spy in U.S. history was retired U.S. Navy Warrant Officer John Walker, Jr. From 1967 until his arrest in 1985, he photographed hundreds of thousands of secret U.S. Navy documents for the KGB. His work was so extensive he earned the dubious distinction of being the first person to wear out a Minox subminiature camera. (The FBI later estimated that it would take more than 250,000 exposures to wear out the shutter of a Minox subminiature.) After Walker's arrest, the FBI discovered his initial instructions from the KGB for photographing documents. They read:

> **B/W Plus-X pan ASA 125**
>
> **1/100th sec**
>
> **1' 6"**
>
> **75–100 w**

The instructions are as accurate today as when they were given to him to use with the diminutive Minox camera. Translated, the instructions read:

> **Use black-and-white Kodak Plus-X film (film speed ASA 125). Set the shutter speed at $1/100$th of a second, and place the front of the lens 18 inches (45 cm) from the document. Light the document with 75- to 100-watt bulbs.**

A3

DISCOVERING COMPUTER PASSWORDS

Most busy executives select their passwords simply because they are easy to remember—the fear of forgetting a password outweighs the concern that a spy may help him- or herself to sensitive files and/or personal information. Here are three techniques for learning any co-worker's password.

When monitoring your target, give yourself a good excuse to be in his vicinity.

(1) **Secretly observe the person entering his or her password.** This technique was developed by members of the RCMP Security Service (the Canadian version of the FBI) during the Cold War and, incidentally, is equally useful for determining safe combinations.

A. Develop a routine that coincides with your target's morning schedule. Whether you are sharing lame Internet jokes or delivering a steaming cup of Starbucks coffee, the idea is to be standing nearby when the target enters the password.

B. Observe one or two keystrokes each day. (Canadian spies call this the Elephant Technique, which is a reference to the old joke, "How do you eat an elephant? One bite at a time.")

C. Create a log of the keystrokes you identify. Note their approximate order and/or where they are typed in the sequence. It helps to develop a subtle observation style and a thorough knowledge of the standard keyboard layout. Be patient, and systematically record your observations.

D. Determine the number of keystrokes. Once you have assembled an assortment of letters that occur somewhere in the password, concentrate on counting the keystrokes.

E. Fine-tune your observations. Once you have the exact number of strokes and an approximate order, the guessing game begins. Most people are so fearful of forgetting a password, they use the names of their children, birthdates, or words from hobbies. Once they create it, few people bother to change it. Test the passwords when your target is out of the office or not logged in; some servers will not permit a user to be logged on in two locations.

Canadian tradecraft instructors who developed and taught this technique learned that a trained observer can reconstruct the average computer password after eight or nine observations. Further experience showed that good typists are better at acquiring the target's keystrokes. Also, the more you know about the personal life of the target, the more likely the assorted letters will make sense.

Some large companies run software that is set to flag repeated unsuccessful attempts to gain access to a password-protected system. Ask your favorite IT guy what might happen if, oh, I don't know, somebody forgets his or her new password and needs to try some combinations. Understanding the computer network's tolerance for password probing will let you experiment with confidence.

(2) **Dust the keyboard to determine the keys used in the password.**

A. Before your target arrives for work, dust a light layer of talcum powder onto his or her keyboard—not enough to be noticeable, but enough to tell if the light dusting of powder has been disturbed by a keystroke.

B. Wait for the target to arrive. Position yourself near the target's office just after he or she logs on to the system.

C. Create a feigned emergency. This crisis should require the target to leave the office for a few minutes. (Maybe the target's red Miata was dinged in the parking lot, or the big boss needs to see him or her urgently, or maybe there's some crazy lady out in the hallway yapping about a paternity suit.) Examine the keyboard closely to determine which keys were touched. You won't know the order of the keystrokes, but you'll know the keys that comprise the password.

And when the target comes back and claims that the Miata is fine, just play dumb. Gee, it must have been some other Miata. . . .

D. Using the different keys, determine the password. You might also save yourself some head-scratching by feeding the random letters into an anagram engine on the Internet to see which words they can form. (Try the Internet Anagram Server; www.wordsmith.org/anagram.) Test the password after your target has left for the day.

A keyboard dusted with talcum powder will "record" the letters and numbers in your target's password.

****

(3) **Install a key logger to track the keystrokes made on the keyboard.**
Though a computer's hard drive may be locked and password-protected, accessories such as the keyboard are unprotected and leave the computer vulnerable to a physical attack. If you can gain access to the target computer for even a few seconds, you can install a small plastic device called a *key logger*—an inch-long, off-white plastic device that connects to the keyboard cable. Key loggers are as easy to find on eBay as velvet paintings of dogs playing poker.

Once installed—the device fits the standard connections perfectly—it appears to be part of the computer's equipment. The key logger then stores the next 32,000 keystrokes typed on the computer. Later, remove the key logger and upload its stored information to your computer. One of the first entries is typically the target's password. (Other entries stored in its 32K memory may reveal the target's e-mails, letters, financial data, *Dr. Who* fan fiction, etc.) After a printout is made, you can delete the memory in the key logger and reinstall it on another computer.

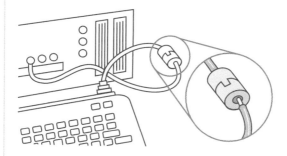

Install a key logger along the wire connecting the keyboard to the computer to track all keystrokes.

A4

ACCESSING YOUR CO-WORKERS' MAIL

There's a letter on your co-worker's desk with an extremely interesting return address. Don't stoop to something so obvious as steaming open the envelope—that's just too messy. Instead, employ this undetectable technique.

(1) **Purchase a can of compressed air.** This stuff is available at most electronics stores; see Appendix E for recommended brands.

(2) **Hold the can upside down and spray the face of the envelope evenly.** Holding the can upside down releases a toxic refrigerant (do not touch it!) that will make the envelope appear translucent for nearly 15 seconds. Once dry, it gives no visual indication that its contents have been exposed. This technique works on almost all types of envelopes, even those made of brown paper. You should have no trouble reading unfolded correspondence such as paychecks and bank deposit slips.

(3) **Take a digital photograph of the envelope if the letter inside is folded.** Here's where things get a little tricky. Really determined spies will take a digital photograph after applying the spray, then try to make creative use of software such as Photoshop to reassemble the jumble of words inside.

A5

RECONSTRUCTING SHREDDED DOCUMENTS

Many businesses rely on shredders that are centrally located on each floor of the office. These machines are usually convenient to no one, and are generally unused except for incredibly sensitive documents. Most executives have no idea what happens to their shredded documents; they believe they've simply been wiped off the face of the earth. Fools. Converting the shredded strips back into complete documents can be done in three steps.

(1)   **Tour the target shredder area at the end of the workday.** Observe how papers are handled and disposed. Many heavy-duty shredders use special plastic bags of a size or color that differentiates them from other waste bags in the office. Identifying this will make recovery of the bags easier later, when you're sorting through the trash. Locate the exterior trash containers where the office's trash is consolidated each night. Plan an after-hours visit to troll for shredded treasure. Recover the bags of shredded material.

(2)   **Reconfigure the strips.** Wear cotton gloves to avoid soiling the strips. Bring the bags of shredded trash to a secure off-site area with large worktables and plenty of space. Only work with one bag at a time. Commingling bags of shredded waste is counterproductive, since the pieces of a single document are always located in the same bag. Open a single bag, and sort the strips into different piles, categorized by the following:

A. Vertical location in the bag

B. Paper size

C. Paper texture

D. Paper color

E. Computer font

(3) **Reconstruct the documents.** Always work in a well-lit area. Manipulate individual strips to form word sequences, using paper weights to hold strips in place. Work slowly and patiently; progress is made one strip at a time. When full pages are recovered, assemble the strips on adhesive sheets and photocopy them.

Scoff if you will, but this method works. After storming the U.S. embassy in 1979, Iranian college students had a field day with the tons of shredded documents they'd collected. The students spent years piecing strips together, and the recovered documents were eventually published by the students to document what they saw as evidence of U.S. imperialism.

 EXPERT TIP: A sophisticated computer program has been developed that scans individual strips, assigns each a number, and then manipulates them within the computer until pages are recovered. It takes powerful computers and plenty of time, but it works. Certain government intelligence security services—we're not going to name names here—are known to have such software.

REASSEMBLING SHREDDED DOCUMENTS

The keys to reassembling a shredded document are a large work-station, plenty of light, excellent eyesight, and lots of patience.

A6

UNCOVERING COMPANY SECRETS

No matter the size of the company, everything important or interesting will be reproduced at some point in the copy room—the master payroll printout, the copy of the disputed credit card bill, the latest performance reviews, *everything*. The challenge is to find an opportunity to access the important stuff without drawing attention to yourself as you rummage through the trash.

(1) **Become friends with the copy-room attendant, if your company has one.** Share lunches, remember birthdays, buy double martinis at a nearby bar, set up dates with single friends—anything to get him or her on your side. Your goal is unfettered access to that room with no questions asked, even if you're peeking at printing jobs in process or trolling through the waste receptacles. After all, you're just visiting your buddy.

(2) **If you cannot befriend the attendant, fabricate an incident that will force the attendant to leave the room.** Phoning in a situation to the main office is the most effective method, because the copy room is not likely to have its own phone. Be sure to use a prepaid calling card at a pay phone to make the call (see Section D1). Try one of the following excuses.

A. Call the main office of your company and identify yourself as a teacher at the school your target's child attends. Explain that there has been a "small problem," provide a fake phone number, and leave a message asking the target to telephone immediately. Do not leave the actual number of the school; a wrong number will distract your target even longer as he or she struggles to sort out the mess.

B. Call the target's office and say you work for building security. Explain that someone has just bumped the attendant's car in the employee parking lot and that the police need him or her to come down immediately.

C. Call the target's office and explain that you're calling from the emergency room of the local hospital. State that there is an injured person asking for the target. Do not identify the person or yourself. Then hang up. Even if your target is fortunate enough to reach someone in the ER, no details will be confirmed over the phone. Your target will have to rush to the emergency room and spend at least an hour attempting to verify that no one he or she knows is hospitalized. You'll be able to put the hour to good use reviewing the data he or she abandoned in the copy room.

(3) **Investigate the trash.** Copy machines have become so complex that something is almost *always* wrong with the first few copies. These get whipped into the trash right away, and they just might contain the information you need. Many senior executives enjoy seeing everything they write reproduced on the color copier, regardless of the extra expense. This kind of foolish indulgence results in more opportunities for you: Color copiers are more temperamental and waste even more paper. If you are not alone in the copy room, explain that you threw away an important document by mistake, and pretend to retrieve it.

(4) **Seek out original documents.** Check the tops of the copy machines; it's possible that a person in a hurry has left an original document resting on the glass. And if the copy room has a tray, file, or folder marked FOR SHREDDING ONLY, by all means go through it. Since these documents are already slated for destruction, no one will miss them. Just abscond with the originals.

(5) **Leave before the copy-room attendant returns.**

A7

MONITORING YOUR CO-WORKERS' HOURS

A co-worker makes a big fuss about staying late every night and doing extra work. But is it true? Sure, you could check the time sheets, but they're about as honest as the expense reports. Some savvy spying in the office parking garage will tell you everything you need to know.

(1) **Buy a cheap windup wristwatch.** Your local flea market should have a wide selection of choices that cost less than five dollars. The wristband doesn't matter; the watch head itself must be in working condition. Use a windup or quartz watch; digital watches will not work for this technique.

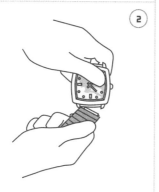

(2) **Remove the wristband.**

(3) **Wrap the watch in a small square of duct tape.** Protect the face from the tape by first covering it with a chewing gum wrapper or other small piece of paper.

(4) **Locate the target's car.** As you're leaving work at the end of the day, place the duct-tape-wrapped watch beneath the right rear tire of the employee's car.

(5) **The next morning, recover the duct-tape-wrapped watch.** The position of the hands will tell you the precise time your target left the previous night. Since it looks like a regular piece of duct tape, it won't attract any attention from passersby.

A8

COVERTLY RECORDING MEETINGS YOU ATTEND

Wish you had a memory like a tape recorder (especially when your co-worker says something very embarrassing about Old Ironbutt, your boss)? You won't have to after you prepare for impromptu meetings with this simple spy trick.

(1) **Prepare your equipment.** Establish a separate telephone number at home, then connect it to an answering machine that automatically records all incoming messages of any length—without beeping.

The microphone in a typical cell phone is capable of recording all of the audio in a room.

(2) **Program your home number to a speed-dial key on your cell phone.**
Be sure the phone is fully charged.

(3) **Set your cell phone to silent mode to prevent it from ringing.**

(4) **Bring your cell phone to the meeting.**

(5) **Make a show of turning off the cell phone as you surreptitiously
press the speed-dial key for home.** Place the cell phone face down
on the table or desk in front of you. By this time, the call will have
connected, and you will be recording the conversation in the room.

EXPERT TIP: The microphone in a typical cell phone is capable of
recording all of the room's audio during a meeting. If you are uncer-
tain about the quality of your cell phone, test the signal strength in
the meeting room *before* the meeting.

A9

COVERTLY RECORDING MEETINGS YOU CANNOT ATTEND

Every businessperson has wished, at one time or another, to be a fly on the wall inside an office where key negotiations (or salary reviews, or staff cuts, or that incompetent moron, Jenkins) are being discussed. Here is a technique that will put you on that wall, even if you weren't invited.

(1)   **Obtain a standard lockable attaché case.** Not too flashy—something in keeping with your business position.

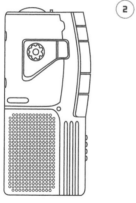

(2)   **Purchase a microcassette recorder.** It should be battery-powered with outlets for an external microphone and a remote on/off switch, and a built-in feature called voice actuation (VOX). This means that the tape recorder activates at the sound of a voice and continues for only a few seconds after the last sound it picks up.

(3)   **Purchase a microphone.** It should be battery-operated with a 70–16,000 Hz response. The cord should be at least 12 inches long with an 1/8-inch plug.

4 **Modify the attaché case.** Tape the microphone to the inside lid of the attaché case. Cut a pinhole-sized opening in an inconspicuous location in the stitching near the microphone, to allow voices and conversation to be picked up clearly. Attach the microphone to the cassette recorder.

5 **Attach the recorder to the inside lid of the briefcase.** A strip of adhesive Velcro will hold it in place. Ideally, the briefcase will have a flap that obscures (or partially obscures) the recorder.

6 **Fill the briefcase lid with folders, documents, and/or a day planner to obscure the recorder.**

(7) **Visit your target.** Make an appointment with your target on the day the off-limits meeting is scheduled to occur (before it begins, of course).

(8) **"Forget" your briefcase.** At some point during your meeting with the target, slip your locked attaché case—with the cassette recorder already in voice actuation mode—beside the target's desk or in some other inconspicuous position.

(9) **At the end of the day, return to pick up your briefcase.** Drop by the office, and explain to the target's assistant that you accidentally forgot your attaché case in the boss's office or conference room.

EXPERT TIP: If an attaché case would be too conspicuous, experiment with hiding your microphone and tape recorder in other objects, such as a thick binder, a laptop case, even a potted plant. (Just make sure you have a likely cover story for later. It might be awkward to march into your boss's office and say, "I've changed my mind! I want the fern back!")

A10

SHADOWING YOUR CO-WORKERS

Following a co-worker you know—and who knows you—without being noticed is more difficult than following a stranger. (A stranger won't suddenly turn around and say, "Chet? Chet Davis from accounts payable? What are you . . . are you *following* me?") These techniques will help you remain undetected while you're tailing that shifty-eyed co-worker during lunch.

(1) **Determine a choke point.** You may not know where your target is headed during lunch, but you do know that he or she will depart from and return to your office location. In most offices, there is one central point that everyone must pass—an escalator, elevator, stairway, entrance to the building, or entrance to the parking lot/garage. In the world of surveillance, this is known as a choke point. Study the layout of your office building to determine the choke point.

When shadowing a co-worker, disguise your appearance by donning a hat and/or changing the style of your clothing.

(2) **Alter your appearance.** Individuals on the street are most often recognized from a distance by a distinctive hat or the color of their clothing. Disguise your appearance by donning a hat and changing the style and color of your outer clothing. (For more elaborate disguise techniques, see Section C3.)

(3) **Always leave the office before, not after, the target (called a "rabbit" by spies).** This way the rabbit is less likely to suspect that he or she is being followed. Leaving first presents you with the opportunity to wait for the rabbit at the choke point.

(4) **Follow the rabbit.** If the rabbit takes a taxi, note the car number and time. You can contact the taxi driver later in the day and—for a mere 20 bucks—purchase the rabbit's exact destination. If the rabbit drives, follow in your own vehicle, staying at least three cars behind. Tail a walking rabbit on foot; keep your distance.

(5) **If you lose sight of the rabbit, don't give up.** Follow the rabbit the next day, and the next, until you have a feel for the destination and can navigate the route easily. If there's clandestine business going on, chances are the rabbit will be going to the same place regularly.

(6) **"Tag" the rabbit.** New advances in global positioning systems (GPS) make it easy and surprisingly inexpensive—often less than $500—to tag a rabbit with a small GPS receiver. This device can be hidden on the rabbit's vehicle; after it's recovered, you can upload the rabbit's exact movements to your computer. The difficulty is in concealing the GPS receiver in a way that allows it to receive the needed signals from the satellites while remaining undetected.

EXPERT TIP: While traveling on foot, professional surveillance specialists usually work in teams of three. The person closest who can see the rabbit "has the eye." The second person follows directly behind the eye, and the third person follows across the street. If the rabbit doubles back or makes a turn, the surveillance team readjusts itself accordingly. The cardinal rule is never to make eye contact with the rabbit. Once that happens, the team member is "burned" and must be replaced.

SECTION B
SECURING YOUR WORKSPACE

BOOBY-TRAPPING YOUR BRIEFCASE

There is a simple trick that will reveal if someone has helped him- or herself to your ideas while you were busy in the executive washroom. And it doesn't require expensive laser-beam alarms or motion detectors— just a few supplies that cost less than 30 cents.

(1) **Obtain three empty, plastic film canisters.** It's best to differentiate them—apply dots of correction fluid or colored stickers, which can be found in any office.

(2) **Place your briefcase on a flat surface with the lid open.** Arrange the film canisters in three predetermined positions in your briefcase. It doesn't matter where, as long as the canisters are upright and you remember their exact locations. This only works if you have a briefcase with a hard shell that lies flat. (If you use a soft bag with handles that sits upright or, even worse, a schoolbag, it's time to trade up.)

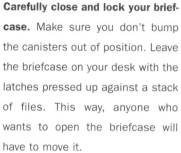

(3) Carefully close and lock your briefcase. Make sure you don't bump the canisters out of position. Leave the briefcase on your desk with the latches pressed up against a stack of files. This way, anyone who wants to open the briefcase will have to move it.

(4) Go about your business.

(5) Upon your return, carefully unlock and open your briefcase. If the canisters have moved at all, someone has tampered with your case. It is nearly impossible to pick the lock of your case without disturbing the three canisters. Even if your office intruder succeeds, he or she will not suspect that you've laid a trap, since film canisters are common, everyday objects.

When the new U.S. Embassy building in Moscow was being constructed in the 1980s, Navy Seabees (construction specialists) were brought in to monitor the movements of the Russian workers, some of whom were thought to be KGB spies. One Seabee considered himself an expert in the field of espionage—after all, he'd read nearly every James Bond novel. He suggested to his fellow Seabees that each day, while they were working at the embassy site, the KGB was entering their hotel rooms and searching their luggage. So the clever Seabee devised a trap: He rigged a piece of luggage with a can of shaving cream that would discharge on the person attempting an unauthorized opening.

At the conclusion of work that day, he and his colleagues rushed back to his room to see if the trap had worked. And it had. The suitcase was partially open, and shaving cream was all over the place. While congratulating himself for outwitting the KGB, the Seabee detected an odd odor. He opened his luggage and discovered that someone had defecated on his packed clothes. *Moral of the story:* Never claim to know spy shit unless you really do.

B2

SECURING YOUR TRASH

If someone gains access to your trash, eventually that person will know everything about you. Seemingly innocuous pieces of discarded paper, collected over time, allow interested individuals to piece together a complete profile of almost anyone. In the words of one seasoned American counterintelligence specialist: "If I have regular, unfettered access to your trash, you have no secrets."

(1) **For more secure removal, skip the shredder and procure a "burn bag."** If something must be effectively and irrevocably destroyed, you must burn it. Keep a burn bag close to your desk or your secretary's desk. A burn bag isn't a fancy gizmo that incinerates everything inside with a mere pull of a rip cord; it's simply a way to keep all of your to-be-destroyed documents in a single place. Your burn bag should be easily accessible but never too obvious. A gym bag makes a convenient and discreet burn bag.

(2) **Throughout your day, place sensitive materials inside the burn bag.** If you leave your office, lock the burn bag in your safe or desk drawer.

(3) **Remove your burn bag from the office every night.** If you are worried that you might leave the burn bag behind, place your car keys in it—you'll never leave for home without them, or without the trash.

(4) **Burn the documents thoroughly, and scatter the ashes.** Pick your favorite burning method—throw them in your BBQ pit; toss them into a basement furnace; dump them into a steel drum you keep in the back yard to burn leaves. Keep in mind that thick manuals and books must be torn apart before burning; the absence of oxygen between the pages acts as insulation. While the outside may char, the inside pages can often withstand the heat of a furnace. Scatter the ashes in an inconspicuous place—on the compost heap, in the bottom of the fireplace, or along a dirt road.

 EXPERT TIP: If you shred documents, use a "crosscut" shredder. The standard "strip" shredder cuts a document into 40 strips that may vary (by model) between $1/16$th and $1/8$th of an inch ($1/3$ to $1/6$ cm). The strips could be pieced back together by an enterprising infiltrator (see Section A5). A crosscut shredder will transform your most private documents into heaping piles of confetti.

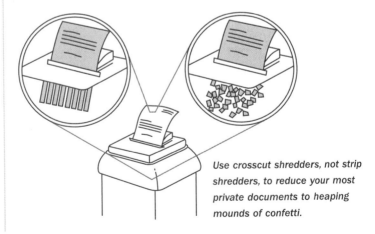

Use crosscut shredders, not strip shredders, to reduce your most private documents to heaping mounds of confetti.

SPIES AT WORK

Aldrich Ames is remembered as the most damaging spy in the history of the CIA. He was arrested in 1994 after nine years of spying for the KGB and the SVR. And he might never have been stopped if the FBI hadn't analyzed his garbage.

In the wee hours of the morning on trash days, a black, unmarked FBI van would appear and discreetly remove his trash. One night in late 1993, searchers found several bits of a torn-up yellow Post-it note with details of a clandestine meeting. Armed with this evidence of spy trade-craft, the courts quickly issued warrants to allow the secret entry and search of his home, basement office, and computer. They hit pay dirt, recovering even more evidence that Ames was actually a mole for the Soviets and, later, the Russians. He was arrested on February 24, 1994.

B3

PROTECTING YOUR MAIL

You might worry about your e-mail being read by corporate spies. But don't just assume your old-fashioned snail mail is safe. Your most cunning rivals will know how to infiltrate your envelopes. Here's how you can tell if someone has been tampering with your mail.

OUTGOING MAIL

(1) **Slip carbon paper inside your letter before placing it in the envelope.** The piece of carbon paper should be slightly smaller than the size of the envelope and undetectable once it's placed in the folded letter. If an attempt is made to manipulate the sealed envelope with "dry flap manipulation"—using tools to slowly open a flap that is not well sealed—the tool marks will leave scratches on the letter from the carbon paper.

(2) **Add a few grains of Kool-Aid to the envelope.** Attempts at "wet flap manipulation" (using steam to loosen the flap glue or carbon tetrachloride to remove cellophane tape) will dissolve the Kool-Aid and leave a stain on the paper inside. To be certain that the grains of Kool-Aid are near the flap, place a piece of double-sided tape on the inside of the flap, just inside the gum line. Cover the exposed side of the tape with dry Kool-Aid granules.

INCOMING MAIL

Examine the sides of the envelope with an ultraviolet (UV) light. The oldest known method of reading the contents of a sealed envelope is called the "French opening." This technique involves cutting a small, 1/8-inch (1/3-cm) slit in the lower corner of the envelope, then inserting two small, metal rods and rolling the letter around them. Once rolled, the letter is removed through the slit and read or photographed. Afterward, it is reinserted and unrolled, and the slit is resealed with a small touch of glue. To detect this technique, examine all envelopes visually as well as with a small UV light—many types of glue will fluoresce under UV light.

If you fear that someone has tampered with your mail, study the envelope under an ultraviolet light.

EXPERT TIP: Most professionals use thinned Elmer's Glue, which does not fluoresce under a UV light.

B4

PROTECTING YOUR INTERNET AND E-MAIL ACTIVITY

Is your boss keeping track of how many times you log on to a particular Web site? If you're even asking, the answer is almost certainly yes. The vast majority of firms do some form of monitoring of phone calls, voice mail, Internet usage, and e-mail (estimates are as high as 80 percent among Fortune 500 companies). Assume all e-mails and Internet usage are being monitored by your employer, and take the following protective steps.

(1) **Never download sexual material at work.** Files from pornographic sites are stored in your temp folder, which can be accessed by anyone. Avoid incorporating the word "sex" or any sexual terms in any e-mail or voice mail. Being labeled an abuser of sexual sites on the Internet could earn you special observation, intense surveillance, and/or funny looks in the executive washroom.

(2) **Bring a laptop from home.** Setting up an independent Web-based e-mail service provides some protection from an employer's monitoring, but as long as you access it using the company Internet server, you're still vulnerable. If you must communicate securely on the Internet while at work, bring along your laptop with its own modem, and use a dial-up connection to send and receive e-mails. Be sure to avoid your employer's ISDN line, intranet, or ISP. Your Internet usage should be completely isolated from the company system and prying eyes. If a colleague asks about the presence of your personal

laptop, just say it contains a special software program that you need for a project.

(3) **Encode your correspondence.** If you absolutely must communicate with a conspirator using your office computer, employ word substitution to obfuscate the true meaning of your exchange. For example, the message, "Meet me at the Starlight Motel at 10:00 A.M. on Wed. October 13" could be expressed as, "The Simpson report is due on April 19 at 10:00 A.M." In this example, the sender and the recipient have agreed in advance to use certain codes and coefficients: "Simpson report" is a preset code name for the Starlight Motel. The sender always adds six to all dates, and the receiver always subtracts six from all dates: October, the 10th month, is advanced by six months to April, and the 13th is advanced by six days to the 19th. The receiver reverses the process to translate the actual dates. This technique was utilized by FBI special agent Robert Hanssen, one of the most damaging moles in U.S. history, when he communicated with his KGB and SVR handlers.

B5

SAFEGUARDING YOUR COMPUTER

Computer passwords are like the bottles of Scotch in your desk—they should be replaced at least every 30 days. The more important the information you are protecting, the more frequently the password should be changed.

(1) **Choose a password with multiple elements.** Make sure your password uses the four basic elements of every standard keyboard: lowercase letters, uppercase letters, numbers, and symbols.

(2) **Never use passwords containing words that can be found in a dictionary.** Letter sequences should be selected at random to defeat password-hacking software that utilizes words found in a standard dictionary.

(3) **Make your password as long as possible.** The minimum length for any password should be eight characters, or the maximum length allowed by your software program.

Examples of bad passwords are:

December 14   12345689   marylovesjohn   451-35-2864

An example of a good password is:

1Jnc/*py3?NzW8%

(4) **Use two hands to type in your password.** Make sure no one else is within visual range of your keyboard. Employ a protective technique

by entering your password with one hand while the other hand shields the keystrokes. This is a slow process, but the safety is worth the inconvenience.

(5) **Never log on in a public place.** The chances of being observed are too great. Also, avoid using public access computers in a library, business center, or cyber café. Public access computers are often equipped with surveillance software that can record or otherwise compromise sensitive information. (In 2002, Air Force Sergeant Brian P. Reagan was charged with attempting to contact members of the Iraqi intelligence service to sell secret U.S. satellite information using a public access computer terminal in a northern Virginia library. Special surveillance software tripped him up, leading to his arrest and eventual conviction in 2003.)

(6) **Never write down your password.** If it absolutely must be written down to protect against a faulty memory, the note should be protected inside a sealed envelope inside a safety deposit box or your most secure safe. Alternatively, use a secret writing technique (see Section D7).

B6

BOOBY-TRAPPING SENSITIVE DOCUMENTS

There is a direct correlation between the number of copies made of secret project materials and loss of security: The more copies that exist, the greater the likelihood that one will slip out. At all stages of a sensitive project, identify the absolute minimum number of people who need to retain printed copies of the document. Pass out copies of your sensitive material in meetings, but distribute them in large, bound notebooks that are numbered, individually assigned, and have no loose pages. Binders should be inventoried, handed out at the beginning, and turned in at the end.

If you know in advance that certain individuals need to take binders away from the meeting room, use this "trapping" method to protect yourself against leaks.

(1) **Add a deliberate spacing error on the second page of each person's binder.** For example, if the binder is number 024, insert a deliberate extra space after the 24th word on the second page. For binder 025, insert an extra space following the 25th word on the second page. This requires each person to have a special page printed in his or her binder, but with word-processing technology, this is easily accomplished.

(2) **If the information is leaked, and copies of the binder appear elsewhere, check the page you trapped.** The number will lead you to the binder number, which in turn will lead you to your leak.

Note: There is a deliberate spacing error on page 48. Based on the example just described, which binder would be identified? We've hidden the answer on page 166.

SPIES AT WORK

During the Cold War, the internal security service of East Germany, the Stasi, ruled with an iron fist. A problem arose in the early 1970s when the president of East Germany, Walter Ulbricht, received a picture of himself, clipped from East Germany's major communist newspaper, with the words "BIG FAT PIG" written across his face. He received similar clippings virtually every time his photograph appeared in the newspaper. The only clue to the location of the culprit was that the letters were all postmarked from Dresden.

Deciding he could no longer tolerate it, Ulbricht let the Stasi loose. First, an article was planted on the front page of the party newspaper with Ulbricht's picture featured prominently. Then the entire shipment of newspapers destined for Dresden was trapped by printing a unique number, in invisible secret ink, on the reverse of Ulbricht's picture. Each number was then linked in a database to an individual recipient assigned to receive that specific paper. When the next "BIG FAT PIG" clipping arrived, it was turned over to the Stasi, who quickly developed the secret ink on the reverse and discovered that the number was linked to the address of the local secretary of the communist party in Dresden—and one of Ulbricht's political rivals: Big fat *oops.*

B7

SECURING YOUR HOTEL ROOM

A businessperson staying in a hotel needs three things: a decent gym, a well-stocked mini-bar, and privacy. (Otherwise, you'd have stayed with a relative.) But your privacy could be compromised if a corporate rival knows where you're staying and, more important, knows how to break into your room while you're sweating away on the StairMaster.

(1) **Check into your room under an assumed name.** Create a fictional identity, and support it with a credit card issued in the new name. Sure, a credit card company will verify your personal identification, address, and financial information as part of the process of issuing a card, but these companies also allow cardholders to request additional credit cards on the primary cardholder's account. The name on the secondary card can be your spouse, a family member, or any other name you provide. (Banks have no financial risk, since the primary cardholder guarantees all charges made using a secondary card.) Make the reservation in your new name, using the corresponding card. Once the card is validated, you will be welcomed as a guest.

(2) **Convert your room into a safe haven.**

A. Avoid accepting a room on the ground floor. Illegal entry through a ground-floor door or window is much easier. Avoid any room that opens directly onto a parking lot and any room that shares a common balcony with another room.

B. Never take the elevator directly to your floor. Always go to a floor that's one or two levels above or below your actual floor and then take the stairs to your floor.

C. Never give out your room number.

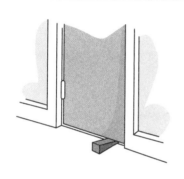

D. Carry small rubber door-wedges while traveling. The primary threat of hostile entry by a professional will come from the interior door leading to the adjacent hotel room (if there is one). Secure all entry doors with a small wedge whenever you are inside your room.

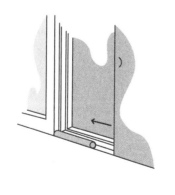

E. Carry a "charlie bar" while traveling. This bar should be wedged onto the open track at the bottom of any exterior sliding door. An improvised wedge can be constructed from a length of dowel or a rubber wedge jammed into the track. Or use a self-tapping screw and drive it in, next to the sliding-door frame to block the track.

F. **Secure the windows.** If you are forced to take a room on the ground floor and the windows aren't outfitted with secure locks, prevent them from opening by inserting a small, self-tapping metal screw into the frame above the bottom pane. This will jam the track and prevent the window from opening.

G. **Cover the peephole.** Place a small piece of tape over the interior side of the peephole in the main door. Otherwise, any spy with a reverse imaging optical viewer could monitor your behavior without your knowledge.

H. **Unplug the phone.** The easiest way for a competitor to eavesdrop is to modify (tap) the telephone instrument in your room. Your phone calls will be overheard, and even if the instrument is not in use, any conversations in the room will be monitored. To prevent this, always unplug the phone when it is not in use. If you must make an important call, use a pay phone located away from the hotel.

I. **Utilize "sound masking" in the room to make eavesdropping more difficult.** The simplest method is to turn the television set on with the volume at a moderate level. When conversing with someone, whisper or talk in very soft voices. Anyone attempting to monitor your conversations will struggle to pick up a signal and filter out the extraneous noise. Be aware that, given enough hidden microphones strategically placed around the room, even this method of sound masking can be defeated. Create a "jabber tape" to counteract diligent eavesdroppers (see Section D4).

J. **If you are not sound masking, keep the TV unplugged.** Most televisions are positioned facing the bed; they are popular places to conceal a hidden microphone or embedded pinhole video camera, which can run off the TV's power cord.

K. **Only allow the hotel cleaning crew in your room when you are present.** Request that your room be cleaned in the mornings while you work at the desk. When you leave the room, always place the "Do Not Disturb" sign on the outside of the door, and leave the television on at medium volume.

(3) **Rig an alarm on your hotel room door.** Before retiring for the night, position a desk chair in front of— and physically touching—all entry doors. On the seat of the chairs, build a small pyramid of three empty water glasses from the bathroom. Balance the glasses so they are stable but will be dislodged by any movement of the door. If an intruder attempts to force the door, your rubber door-wedges will keep the door secure, and the movement will trip the water-glass alarm system.

B8

HIDING SENSITIVE PAPERS WHILE TRAVELING

While on a business trip, there are times when confidential material or valuables must be left in your hotel room. Though many hotel rooms now contain small safes with removable keys, you should not use these. The keys are almost never changed and, once copied, can be used by anyone who can access your room. The most common hiding places for valuables are the first places a burglar will look. Never hide valuables in your luggage, inside your shoes, under the mattress, inside the pillow-case, behind the television set, or inside clothes hanging in the closet. Try this method instead.

(1) **Obtain a large plastic freezer bag.** Fill it with your jewelry, wallet, money clip, the secret formula for Coke, and any other confidential materials in your possession.

(2) **Stand on a chair near the drapes.** Using a large safety pin, attach the bag to the reverse side of the drapes in your room. Place the bag near the very top, where the drapes are suspended from the rod, between the sheer and the drape, or even inside the folds of the drape.

(3) **Make sure the safety pin and bag aren't visible from outside the window or inside the room.** Positioned in this manner, your stash will be almost impossible to find, and it will be overlooked by the average burglar or hotel employee.

EXPERT TIP: Given enough time, professional thieves can find *anything* that you have hidden. But because time is always limited, they are more likely to search the logical hiding places. If nothing is soon found, they'll move on.

Pin your belongings to either end of the drapes. This limits telltale rustling if your thief opens the curtains, and ensures the package is not visible from outside.

89

SAFEGUARDING A MEETING

The annual marketing meeting is in three days. Now, this isn't any old marketing meeting; this is the King Daddy of marketing meetings, where next year's products and advertising campaign will finally be unveiled. Your competition would do almost anything to be there.

And they just might.

Audio eavesdropping, or "bugging," is one of several tools used by corporate spies to secretly "gather" (read: "steal") important information about a competitor. The reason for such sneaky tactics? They work. Obtaining an advance peek into a competitor's marketing strategy can save millions in advertising dollars. When millions are at stake, and information must be protected, a professional ECM (electronic counter-measures) specialist should be brought in to sweep your meeting room. (See Appendix E for a recommended professional.) If that isn't an option, the following steps are the next best things.

(1) **Don't leave your office building.** Instead of booking space in a hotel or convention center, arrange the meeting in a room or facility that you or your company controls.

(2) **Secure the perimeter.** If any other company shares a common wall with the meeting room, don't use that room. A common wall is an ideal place for a competitor to place a listening device. Ditto for the space on the floors above or below your meeting room.

(3) **Limit attendance to key personnel.** More people = less security.

(4) **Prohibit electronic recording devices.** Who knows where the authorized recording may surface? Also discourage coats and briefcases, which can be used to conceal tape recorders.

(5) **Prohibit cell phones.** Asking people to turn off cell phones isn't enough; these devices shouldn't be anywhere near a confidential meeting. (Mossad, the Israeli intelligence service, used to require guests to place cell phones on the table and remove the batteries. Mossad officers did the same thing. Later, it was discovered that the Mossad had built special listening devices into the cell phone batteries. After the meeting, Mossad officers would pop the battery back in, and the phone would automatically dial a designated phone number to upload the conversation.)

(6) **Remove all other electronic appliances.** Traditional telephones, video players, televisions, A/V projectors, and coffeemakers are all excellent places to hide microphones. If the appliance is built in— or too heavy to move—at least make sure it's unplugged. Many tiny bugs leach off the power supply of the appliance. Even a phone outlet carries about 60 volts, which is more than enough to power a small listening device.

(7) **Remove all trash receptacles and potted plants.** These objects are commonly used to conceal microphones. Beware of newly arrived flowers that congratulate your company on its latest success. Never allow last-minute gifts or décor pieces to be added after the room has been searched. (Remember the Trojan horse?)

(**8**)   **Never use wireless microphones.** You'll learn how spies can receive signals transmitted by wireless microphones in Section C7.

(**9**)   **Ensure that the room is soundproof.** Prior to the meeting, play a radio or television in the meeting room at a normal volume level, close the meeting room door, and walk outside the room to test for "acoustical leakage." If you can hear the TV, change rooms to one with less leakage.

(**10**)   **Sweep the room for bugs.** See Section B10.

BIO

DEBUGGING A MEETING ROOM

In companies throughout the United States, more than 85 percent of all discovered listening devices are found as a result of a thorough physical search. The good news is that you can do your own search, even without the aid of an electronic countermeasures specialist.

(1) **Closely examine the ceiling.** If the meeting room has removable ceiling tiles, remove several and search the area above them with a flashlight. Look for any electronic-looking devices or microphones concealed overhead. Be especially suspicious of any small wires that disappear into the ceiling tiles or run behind the walls. Cut any wires that seem unnecessary.

Check for small, thin wires running over ceiling panels.

(2) **Cut the music.** Disconnect any Muzak or other built-in loudspeakers used for background music or announcements. A speaker can easily be transformed into a microphone by changing the wiring.

(3) **Examine each piece of furniture.** Search the top, bottom, and sides of all bookcases, upholstered pieces, tables, desks, and chairs. Look for wooden furniture components that appear to have been recently added, repaired, or replaced; these could contain a hidden listening device.

(4) **Search all wall outlets, including electrical, telephone, data, and control circuits.** Look carefully for any added electronic components lurking behind the outlet plates.

(5) **Search the floor area.** Pay special attention to any floorboards that appear recently repaired; these might conceal a microphone or electronic listening device. Scan the area with an ultraviolet light; newly applied paint concealing listening devices will be visible.

(6) **Unplug and remove any hardwired telephones.** These instruments may have been modified to eavesdrop on conversations.

SPIES AT WORK

During the early years of the Cold War, two aggressive young U.S. State Department security officers were sent to Vienna, Austria, to observe the first postwar meeting of U.S. ambassadors from western European countries. Forewarned of the aggressive tactics used by the KGB at the nearby Soviet embassy, the young security officers requested a suite of rooms directly above the grand meeting room in the luxury hotel that was chosen as the meeting site.

Their first task was a thorough search for hidden listening devices; after all, just one year earlier, a strange listening device had been found concealed in a carved wooden seal at the U.S. ambassador's residence in Moscow. Under the rugs in the suite, the officers discovered a large brass object embedded in the floor—positioned directly over the meeting room below.

The two worked through the night to remove the object. With the aid of a tool kit retrieved from the nearby U.S. embassy, they finally pried the mysterious device from the floor. It appeared to be nothing but a large threaded brass rod, but they were certain that technicians in Washington could use x-rays to identify the components of the bug inside.

As they descended the main stairway, they glanced toward the grand meeting room and observed a great commotion. A giant 125-year-old crystal chandelier, personally presented to the hotel by Ludwig I of Bavaria, had fallen from the ceiling and crashed to the floor.

The meeting took place the next day, but in a different hotel, and without the young security officers, who were quietly escorted out of the country.

DETECTING A PHONE TAP

Forget the rumors about hearing clicks, snaps, crackles, and pops—even if your eavesdropper uses bargain-basement tapping gear, you'll never hear any telltale noise on the line. And if any branch of the U.S. government (FBI, DEA, IRS, etc.) decides to tap your phone, you'll have no way of finding a physical clue. The feds tap the line at the telephone company, which makes it impossible to detect. So if Uncle Sam is spying on you, you're out of luck.

The good news is that you *can* detect a tap if a nongovernmental source is listening in on your conversations. But it will take some work.

(1) **Check all of your wall-mounted phone jacks.** A lazy spy attaches a device that plugs into an unused wall jack and sends the conversations to a tape recorder or listening device. You'll see a small box with two wires coming out of it. One line plugs into the wall; the other goes into a tape recorder. The circuit in the tap is triggered when someone picks up a phone to answer it or to place a new call. That activates the tape recorder, which automatically stops when the phone is hung up.

(2) **Check the junction box in your office.** Chances are, your company uses one of those fancy digital phone systems. It is difficult to tap directly into one of these. But every digital system connects with an analog line that leads to the phone company, and analog lines are easy to tap. In some office buildings, the junction box is located in a telephone closet that is openly available to anyone who looks. Find

your junction box, and look for suspicious devices connected to it or wires that seem out of place.

(3) **If you find a tap, do nothing.** Think about it. You find a tap and rip it out. The person who is monitoring you will realize something has gone wrong and will simply come up with a more sophisticated way to monitor you. Instead, you should leave the tap in place and proceed to have some fun. Plant disinformation. Tell lies. Send the other party on a wild goose chase. Most important, discuss nothing of value or importance via telephone until you can be confident that you are no longer under active surveillance.

(4) **Don't assume your home is safe.** Eager spies may have infiltrated your home office. Here the phone lines are much simpler—and much more vulnerable. A home phone line is usually a single cable with four internal wires (red, green, yellow, and blue). In a home with just one line, only the red and green are used—the yellow and blue are spares, in case an additional line is needed later. Spies can connect simple equipment to the red and green wires, allowing them to listen to your conversations. Check them for strange-looking devices.

B12

CONCEALING OBJECTS IN A WATER BOTTLE

Where's the last place someone would look for a hidden object? Your contact-lens case, maybe—but that will only work if you're hiding two croutons. A much better option is to rig a bottle of designer water. Water bottles are ubiquitous on the modern desk, much as overflowing ashtrays used to be. Here's how to create a hiding spot that can be left in plain sight with little chance of anyone examining it more carefully.

(1) **Buy two identical, unopened water bottles.** Be sure to select a brand that is commonly available and has a firm plastic bottle.

(2) **Open and drain the contents of one bottle.**

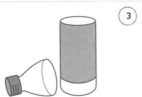

(3) **Using a knife or scissors, carefully trim away the top section of the bottle just above the label.** Be careful not to cut off any part of the label. Discard the top section.

(4) **Take a clear plastic lens from a flashlight, and drill a small hole in the center.** Trim the edge of the lens so it is slightly smaller than the diameter of the bottle. Fit the lens in the bottle so it rests half an inch (1.3 cm) above the bottom of the label.

(5) **Glue the sides of the lens in place with a clear waterproof sealant, such as the type used in plumbing.** Fill the bottom with water, leaving a small amount of space so that, when tipped over, a bubble will appear. Close the drilled opening with sealant. This is the bottom section.

(6) **Using a knife or scissors, cut an opening at the bottom of the second (unopened) bottle.** Drain the bottle.

(7) **Using a knife or scissors, carefully trim away the bottom section of the bottle.** Make the cut one inch (2.5 cm) below the top of the label. Discard the bottom part and remove the label from the top part.

(8) **Take another clear plastic lens from a flashlight, and drill a small hole in the center.** Trim the edge of the lens so it is slightly smaller than the diameter of the bottle. Fit the lens into the top of the bottle; it should rest half an inch (1.3 cm) above the bottom edge.

(9) **Glue the sides of the lens in place with clear waterproof sealant.** Fill the top section with water, but leave about half an inch (1.3 cm) or so for air. Close the drilled opening with sealant. This will be the top section.

(10) **Using one-inch (2.5 cm) sections of clear tape, cover the cut edge of the top section.** Work the tape all around the edge—this will allow the top bottle section to slip easily into and out of the bottom section. It will also help to create a seal and keep the two sections together when in use.

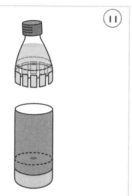

(11) **Fill the bottom section, behind the label, with your sensitive items.** Place some sort of padding—toilet paper or bubble wrap—around your hidden item to dampen any noise or prohibit its movement.

(12) **Carefully ease the top section *into* (not *over*) the bottom section.** Making a half-inch (1.3 cm) vertical cut in the top section will help it slide more comfortably into the bottom section.

BI3

ENCRYPTING YOUR ADDRESS BOOK

While locks, keys, and safe-deposit boxes can protect many types of valuables, a businessperson also needs foolproof methods to keep information secure from prying eyes—but available for use at all times. Such information includes the important contact names and numbers in your Rolodex, Day-Timer, or PalmPilot. Sophisticated encryption programs are available, but the following techniques (while less secure) are inexpensive and practical.

(1) **Assign your important contact a code name.** The code name must have no intuitive link to the real name. Avoid the temptation to select a name that is easily associated with the project. (For example, if your advertising agency is angling for the next *Star Wars* flick, don't use the code name Master Yoda.) Many intelligence agencies randomly generate code names using a computer data bank of a million or more names. You can approximate the same activity by purchasing a book of baby names. Open the book to any page, drop your finger, and use the name closest to it. Gender means nothing when selecting a name for an asset. "Carlos" may be the name for a female, and "Mary" may be the name for a male.

(2) **Change the code name periodically.** Frequently changing names adds to the security of your project, assets, and contacts. Every organization should have only one document that links the names of assets with code names; this document should be sealed and placed inside your most secure safe or in a safe-deposit box.

(3) **Encrypt your contact's phone number.** Select a personal number (PN) that's easy to remember—such as your first high school boyfriend's phone number or Marilyn Monroe's measurements. Don't feel obligated to make your PN seven digits; if you're using fewer digits, simply repeat them until you have seven.

Add the PN to the original telephone number to create an encrypted (safe) number. Note: When adding and subtracting, tens are never carried or subtracted. For example, $8 + 4 = 2$; $3 - 7 = 6$.

Phone number to be encrypted:	3 5 7 - 8 5 1 4
PN to be added:	+ 5 2 9 - 7 5 1 5
Encrypted (safe) number:	8 7 6 - 5 0 2 9

To recover the original number, simply subtract your PN:

Encrypted (safe) number:	8 7 6 - 5 0 2 9
Subtract the PN for recovery:	- 5 2 9 - 7 5 1 5
Original phone number:	3 5 7 - 8 5 1 4

For greater security, assign a different PN to each contact. Begin by numbering the entries in your address book, then turn to the corresponding page number in your local phone book. Take the first telephone number on the page, and use it as the PN for the number to be encoded. With this technique, each number in your address book is encoded with a different PN; even if one is compromised, the technique still protects the remaining numbers on your list. All you have to do is retain the original telephone book used to select the PNs.

SPIES AT WORK

When East Germany dissolved, the human assets—i.e., spies—who were working for the HVA (East Germany's foreign intelligence service) were left out in the cold. Every spy had a code name, but who had possession of the master list linking the code names to the real names? The search for the list was under way even as the East German government dissolved. After much international intrigue, including briberies and deaths, the so-called Rosewood Papers were obtained by the United States. With this information, numerous East German spies were identified and eventually arrested around the globe. The mere existence of the papers—and the demand that they be returned to the new German government—has been a hot topic since 1990.

**SECTION C
GATHERING COMPETITIVE
INTELLIGENCE**

C1

GAINING SECRETS FROM THE COMPETITION

As you've learned in Section B2, your business secrets are only as secure as your office's trash can. This is frightening—until you realize that your competitors' secrets are only as secure as their trash, too.

Don't be squeamish about sifting through bales of refuse. A trash cover is a common collection tool used by commercial spies as well as intelligence services around the world. It's popular for two simple reasons—it works, and it's usually legal. (In 1988 the U.S. Supreme Court ruled that once trash is left out to be picked up, there is no expectation of privacy or continued ownership.) A thorough analysis of the material that companies throw away can provide insight into almost any project.

The first step, however, is being in a position to *take* the trash.

(I) **Monitor the office schedule.** A survey of a competitor's workplace just before closing time will often yield information about how regular and special waste (shredded documents and records) are discarded; make an appointment for late in the day to survey and, later, gather the trash. Some small offices take trash directly to an outside Dumpster, while larger offices often hire a cleaning crew to come in after-hours. Either way, you can almost always locate the refuse quickly. Outside cleaning crews work consistently each time they clean an office. Once you determine where they discard office refuse, it will be there each time they clean. When the crew has departed, return for the trash.

2) **Choose your trash wisely.** Sometimes shredded waste is discarded in plastic bags that fit the shredder, which means they will be a different size or color from other trash bags. Target these first, then refer back to Section A5 for instructions on reconstructing shredded documents. Next, look for bags containing small papers and typical office trash.

3) **Collect the trash.** Quickly and quietly transfer the bags from the Dumpster or street into your waiting vehicle. Work with a team, if possible, to speed up the process.

"Dumpster dive" to collect valuable information about your competition's secret projects and future marketing plans.

SPIES AT WORK

In April 2001, Procter & Gamble discovered that some of its employees had hired corporate spies to poke through the Dumpsters of a competitor, Unilever. When P&G executives learned they were bankrolling Dumpster diving, they claimed to be outraged and told Unilever about the incident. Naturally, Unilever was not pleased. P&G proceeded to return the stolen documents—more than 80 of them—and pledged not to use the info, which was largely about Unilever's hair-care product business strategies for the next three years. Unilever did not take P&G at its word, however, and demanded that a third-party auditor examine P&G to make sure it hadn't acted on any of the information. The dispute was finally settled the following September, but not without both companies airing some of their dirty laundry.

C2

CREATING A NEW IDENTITY

We know a well-spoken British businessman who has business cards identifying himself as a gossip columnist. The cards allow him to approach anyone at an event and ask the most probing, and sometimes personal, questions without anyone raising an eyebrow.

The name on your driver's license, the college diploma on your wall, and the number of zeros in your bank account are all irrelevant to strangers. Their assessment of you is determined by how you look, how you speak, and the information printed on your business card. To question people at business events without causing suspicion, simply present the right business card for the situation.

1. **Collect business cards everywhere you go.** Names, titles, and positions mean little. The real value is in the design of the card, the logo of the company, and other specific information on the card. Collect cards at every business function you attend, and ask for a card from everyone you meet. If you visit a restaurant that has a "drop your card for a free lunch" bowl, reach inside and grab a handful. (It's not as if anybody ever wins those things, anyway.)

2. **Create your own cards.** With a computer, scanner, printer, and some nice card stock, you can match fonts, alter a few words, and create business cards from any company or organization of your choice. These days, even enterprising ten-year-olds can create convincing, elegant business cards in 30 minutes or less.

BELMONT SOLUTIONS

ROBERT JORDAN
Senior Grant Analyst

55 Walnut Street
Belmont, NC 28012
Phone: (704) 555-1212
Fax: (704) 555-1313
E-mail: R_JORDAN@ss.com

The Financial Daily

ROBERT JORDAN
Research

55 Walnut Street, Belmont, NC 28012
Phone: (704) 555-1212 Fax: (704) 555-1313
Email: rjordan@findaily.com

Reports, Reviews, and Research from a Team of Economic Experts

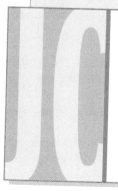

JORDAN CONSULTING

ROBERT JORDAN
Executive Consultant

55 Walnut Street
Belmont, NC 28012
Phone: (704) 555-1212
Fax: (704) 555-1313

(3) **Always carry the appropriate cards.** If your card says you're a researcher/analyst for an industry publication or Web site, you'll have license to ask probing questions about new products, marketing strategies, etc. (Human nature is strange. People will clam up when faced with a competitor but spill the beans to someone in the media.) Examples of other generic titles and positions you may want to adopt: *Business Researcher, Trends Analyst, Business Consultant, Grant Analyst, Investigator, Regional Economic Analyst,* and, of course, *Gossip Columnist.*

(4) **Set up a contact number.** If you include a telephone number on your card, hire an answering service to greet incoming calls with "[Alias Name's] office." The answering service will be unable to specify what your office actually does. As long as you use the same last name, you could conceivably be involved in an unlimited number of companies.

EXPERT TIP: It is a bad idea to identify yourself using different names and positions to individuals attending the same social function; eventually, you'll be discovered.

C3

DISGUISING YOUR APPEARANCE

Sometimes you can't hide behind a business card, especially if you are recognized by sight in your industry. Whether you're attending your competitor's annual meeting, secretly visiting a key test-market, or venturing into the enemy's booth at a trade show, anonymity has value.

Studies have demonstrated that people who see you at a distance will recognize you long before they can identify your face. Individuals have identifying characteristics that they may be oblivious to, but that others can easily recognize.

A person's appearance has the following primary characteristics:

Hair: style, length, color, quantity.

Face: facial hair, physical characteristics, piercings, jewelry, eyeglasses, makeup, wrinkles.

Physique: height, weight, body type, posture, disability, sex.

Gait: the way you walk, stand, or run.

Clothing and footgear: type, style, color, texture.

Accoutrement: body jewelry, tie tacks, lapel pins, belt buckles, rings, bracelets, belts, cigarettes, pipes, gloves.

Accessories: crutches, canes, briefcases, bags, purses, cell phones, beepers, books.

By modifying only a few of these characteristics, you may find that even your closest acquaintances will no longer recognize you.

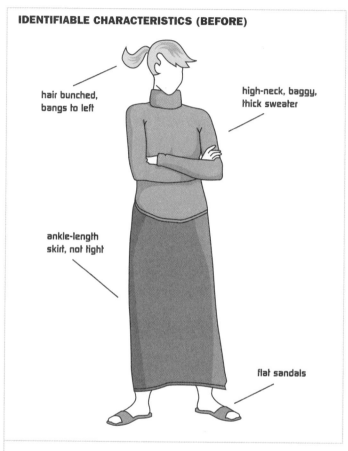

IDENTIFIABLE CHARACTERISTICS (BEFORE)

hair bunched, bangs to left

high-neck, baggy, thick sweater

ankle-length skirt, not tight

flat sandals

1. **Perform a self-analysis.** Using the list on the opposite page, try to see yourself as the rest of the world does. What makes you stand out in a crowd? What are your ten most identifiable characteristics? Pose these same questions to two of your friends. Then pose these questions again to two strangers—one male and one female. In the

end, you'll have five lists to compare. What are the characteristics that most people agree on? Once identified and prioritized, the top five characteristics can be changed to achieve anonymity.

(2) **If time is limited, make a quick fix.** The fastest way to alter your appearance is to change the style and type of your clothing, hair color, and headwear. In recognition studies, these changes have been shown to conceal identity most effectively.

(3) **Work in opposite directions.** If your hair is long, get it cut; if it's short, don a hairpiece. If you're normally clad in Hawaiian shirts, switch to button-downs. If you're wearing a diamond stud in your ear, take it out. If you're short, wear elevator shoes. Exceptions: You can make a person taller, but it is difficult to make someone shorter; you can make a person heavier, but it is difficult to make someone thinner. Otherwise, virtually every identifying characteristic can somehow be changed, concealed, altered, obfuscated, or masked.

(4) **Consider adding a detractor.** This is simply an element of your appearance that is designed to draw attention. When people focus on the detractor, they often overlook many other elements of your appearance. Examples of common detractors include a gold front tooth, thick glasses, a large facial wart, deformed or protruding teeth (think Austin Powers), very large breasts (on a woman, naturally), an unusual cap or hat, a cane, crutches, a monocle, and an eye patch.

DISGUISING YOUR IDENTITY (AFTER)

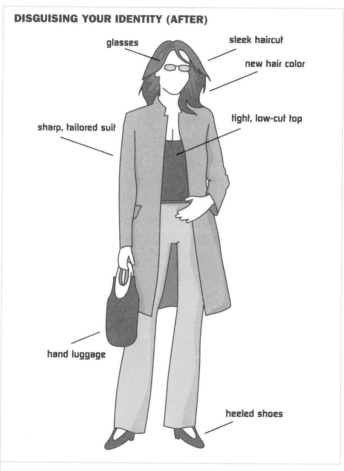

glasses

sleek haircut

new hair color

sharp, tailored suit

tight, low-cut top

hand luggage

heeled shoes

 EXPERT TIP: Use detractors with caution. The goal is to look like someone other than yourself, not to mimic an obscure James Bond villain.

SPIES AT WORK

One classic example of using disguise to escape a hostile situation occurred in early 1980, when legendary CIA technical officer Tony Mendez rescued six U.S. diplomats from Iran. Following the U.S. embassy takeover by radical Iranian students, the Canadian ambassador to Iran, Ken Taylor, hid the six diplomats at a private residence. The clock was ticking, and the diplomats needed to get out quickly. Using his background as chief of disguise for the CIA, Mendez created a fictional Canadian film company (Studio Six Productions) to serve as the cover for the daring rescue operation.

Posing as a filmmaker on a location-scouting mission, he traveled to Tehran using a Canadian passport. He brought disguises and new identities for the stranded diplomats. The disguises altered their appearances slightly by changing their clothing and hairstyle. The hardest part of the operation for Mendez was convincing the diplomats that their new identities—as laid-back filmmakers—would withstand Iran's intensive exit procedures.

In the early morning hours of January 28, 1980, the team traveled to Tehran's Mehrabad airport and prepared to board a Swissair flight to Zurich. After successfully answering questions while passing through the Iranian immigration checkpoints, they reached the departure lounge, only to find that the flight had been delayed due to a mechanical problem. As they waited nervously, members of the Iranian Guard entered the lounge and began asking for travel documents and searching passengers for contraband. Fortunately, their disguises, documentation, and cover held, and the six diplomats reached Zurich safely.

C4

SNEAKING INTO A COMPETITOR'S ANNUAL MEETING

It's the most important event of the business season, and your biggest competitor didn't send you an invite. (How rude!) You certainly don't want to miss out on all of the new technology and marketing plans for the coming year, so here are two easy ways to make a stealth appearance at the big show.

(1) **Secure legitimate credentials.**

A. Identify the waste receptacle closest to the exit. Many people jettison their ID badges as soon as they leave an event. Wait for the crowd to thin, and search the trash for a couple of valid passes.

B. Wear the badge. If you are worried that the name on the pass may be well known, partially obscure it with your clothing.

(2) **Walk right in . . . backward.**

A. Dress appropriately. Wear clothing that won't distinguish you from the other invited attendees. Don't overdress; just blend in with the crowd.

B. Identify the main exit. When the day's events are half over, the exit will be filled with attendees who are leaving early to avoid the rush. Find the exit that is the most crowded.

SNEAKING INTO AN ANNUAL MEETING

Wait until the exit area is filled with people walking out, and slowly walk in backward, letting the crowd pass you by.

c. Back your way in. Simply wait until the exit area is filled with people walking *out,* and slowly walk *in* backward, letting the crowd pass you by. Members of the security detail may be scanning the crowd for people attempting to sneak in—but you won't capture their attention, because you'll be facing the same way as everyone else. From the perspective of the people exiting around you, you will just appear to be walking slowly.

C5

GATHERING COMPETITIVE INTELLIGENCE AT CONVENTIONS

Annual meetings at swank big-city hotel complexes are usually attended by a cast of hundreds, including advertising personnel, creative consultants, outside strategists, franchisees, and clients. There will be so many extraneous and redundant people (this is corporate America, after all) that it will be easy for you to slip in and out of the hotel unnoticed. Once you're inside, here are the best ways to gather intelligence.

(1) **Put yourself in the line of fire.** Conversational fire, that is. Wander around the usual hotel meeting places such as the pool, health club, and lounge. Always be willing, but not overly anxious, to strike up a conversation with attendees.

(2) **If somebody asks, identify yourself as a consultant.** There are so many consultants employed by large companies that most people don't know who they are or what they do. (They're usually hired on a freelance basis so the company doesn't have to incur the full cost of company benefits.) Be prepared, if challenged, to identify yourself using a business card stating that you are a business consultant (see Section C2).

(3) **Dress in a manner consistent with other attendees.** Business casual has become the standard for most meetings, but be prepared with a variety of clothing options. You never know when you might have to duck into a black-tie cocktail party.

(4) **Clean up after your fellow event-goers.** Attendees at most large meetings and conventions are lax about leaving materials behind, especially advertising-agency personnel. Copies of meeting agendas and new marketing campaigns can be picked up in meeting rooms at the ends of presentations. Security guards usually check people *entering* a meeting that's about to begin, not people *reentering* a completed meeting. Just stroll in and pick up all of the agendas and notes you can carry. If questioned, state that you are looking for the "consolidated distributors" meeting. (Simply make up a name: no one, including the hotel staff, really knows the name of every meeting.)

(5) **Hang out near the phones.** Pretend to be busy while you lurk near the pay phones, or outside, where participants with cell phones congregate. Pretend to be working, but secretly take notes. You'll be surprised at what you can hear.

Hang out near pay phones to overhear confidential information.

EXPERT TIP: There is a shared bond among smokers forced to go outside for their nicotine fix. Posing as one of them may yield valuable information.

(6) **Help the hotel cleaning staff.** At the conclusion of a convention, examine the huge carts of trash that are removed by the cleaning staff from each floor. Executives are often too lazy to carry home the bulky and detailed meeting notes—overhead bins are only so big—so they often ditch them in their hotel rooms. Walk the halls after checkout time, and you can pretty much troll for treasure.

SPIES AT WORK

During the Cold War, Soviet journalists were often provided with amazing access to Western industrial complexes. One early goal of Soviet industry was to learn more about the metallurgy used in the U.S. ICBM (intercontinental ballistic missile) program. The KGB gave the journalists special shoes made with soft gum-rubber soles that literally picked samples up off the floors. After departure from the production plant, the shoes were sent back to Moscow. Soviet metallurgists were able to recover enough samples of the filings to perform an accurate spectrographic analysis of the metal. They found what they needed, and Soviet missiles were later built using a very similar lightweight metal.

C6

PRYING TRADE SECRETS OUT OF COMPETITORS

In the world of spies, gathering information through conversation with someone who is unaware that he or she is the target of a "soft interrogation" is known as elicitation. It is one of the most effective and nonthreatening ways to gather information.

Elicitation is a collection of conversational gambits used by ordinary persons in ordinary conversations to gain information without being obvious. Used-car salespeople employ it with customers; fathers use it on their daughters' boyfriends; psychiatrists may use it to extract information from patients. Of course, spies use it, too. Elicitation is hard to recognize as an intelligence technique—after all, this is just a little conversation among friends, right?

(1) **Introduce elicitation techniques.** So there you are, elbows on the bar, deep in conversation with someone who's high up in the ranks of a competing company. How can you steer the conversation toward your topics of interest?

A. Appeal to your target's ego, self-esteem, or prominence.
SPY: *"Sounds like you're quite a player at your company. The way your boss keeps slobbering over you, I was ready to bring him a bib."*
SUBJECT: *(embarrassed laugh) "Oh, please. He's like that with everybody, and my job isn't even that important. What I do is. . . ."*

B. Express mutual interest.

SPY: *"You're a tech geek like me, aren't you? Hey, beam me your e-mail address, and maybe we can swap war stories. You oughta see the Sun workstation I've got at home."*

SUBJECT: *"You're serious? I've always wanted to try one of those suckers. I use a CAD/CAM program, but my computer. . . ."*

C. Make deliberately false statements. These will often produce denials—along with the real facts—from the listener. Most of us have a natural tendency to correct misstatements, to inform others, and to appear to be "in the know."

SPY: *"Aw, c'mon. Everybody knows that the colonel's eleven herbs and spices are listed on the Internet."*

SUBJECT: *"Actually, that isn't true. You know, down at KFC headquarters, we keep the formula hidden beneath. . . ."*

(2) **Fine-tune the technique.** Elicitation requires patience. Don't rush the process. Be content to develop relationships over time, and gradually accumulate bits and pieces of information. Some other points to keep in mind:

A. Make sure you establish a good cover and explanation for why you are having the conversation with the subject. (See Section C2 for advice on creating phony business cards.)

B. Always secretly record your elicitation sessions. Your memory is fallible, but it will look weird if you suddenly start taking notes in a bar. (See Section A8 and A9 for covert recording techniques.)

C. Don't rush things. If your subject detects a sense of urgency, he or she might clam up. Always plan for sufficient time to conduct the conversation.

D. Always listen carefully to the answers the subject provides. Don't be so focused on steering the conversation in one direction that you disregard what the subject is telling you. If the subject senses you have an agenda, the relationship will be in jeopardy.

E. Don't pursue any topic to the point where the subject senses you are becoming aggressive; conversely, don't abandon a topic if the subject is still providing valuable information.

F. If you sense that you've hit a raw nerve with a certain topic, backtrack to a neutral topic, and be patient before attempting to move the conversation back toward the area of perceived sensitivity.

G. Once you've achieved your objective, don't terminate the conversation. Keep talking. Slowly move the discussion to a neutral and nonthreatening topic before ending the conversation.

H. If possible, leave the subject with a positive feeling about the conversation—and a desire to have more discussions in the future.

(3) **Counter any elicitation techniques the competition attempts to use with you.** In every situation, social or professional, there are many legitimate questions that may be asked and answered. Keep in mind, however, that not every conversational gambit is innocent, not every line of conversation needs to be pursued, and not every question needs to be answered. Be mindful at all times that intelligence officers can be any age or sex, and show up in any situation. You have information they wish to collect. You are under no obligation to give it to them. Keep these key principles in mind:

A. You are not obligated to tell this person anything—including personal information about yourself, your colleagues, or your work.

B. You can simply ignore any question you think is improper, and change the topic.

C. You can always deflect the question with one of your own.

D. You can give a nondescript answer.

E. You can simply say you do not know.

F. If all else fails, say flat out that you would have to clear such discussions with your company.

SPIES AT WORK

Richard Tomlinson was recruited into MI6 (the British foreign intelligence service) during his senior year at Cambridge. He served four years before being dismissed in 1995 for reasons that are still somewhat murky. In 2000, Tomlinson published his shocking memoirs in Moscow with the support of the Russian foreign intelligence service.

Among the fascinating details Tomlinson revealed about his secret MI6 training was the focus on conversational skills and field exercises designed to test recruits' skills. One such test, code-named "Perfect Stranger," assigned each recruit to a different pub. The trainees were told to approach a stranger and—using whatever means—learn his or her name, address, occupation, date of birth, and passport number. Each trainee was given an alias and a budget of eight pounds fifty (about $13) for drinks.

Tomlinson befriended two women by posing as a yacht skipper. He invited them to join him for a brief voyage the next day. In order to clear customs at the port, the women provided him with their full contact information and passport numbers. Tomlinson aced the test.

Officer-in-training Richard Tomlinson was a master of conversational skills.

BUGGING A TRADE-SHOW EVENT

Whether they know it or not, many speakers who address large meetings or conventions are wearing secret transmitters. That's because speakers like to roam the stage without the constraints of a fixed microphone. To accomplish this, audio techs will equip each speaker with a small, wireless microphone clipped onto a lapel or worn like a tie clip. The microphone picks up the speaker's voice and transmits it to a receiver at the back of the room. This audio system broadcasts the sound, allows the speaker to pace around like a stand-up comedian—and lets you hear every word without being in the room.

(1) **Obtain a radio scanner.** The speaker's voice signal will probably be broadcast in the 300 MHz frequency range—any good scanner set to "roam and search" for signals will pick it up quickly.

(2) **Test your equipment.** Speakers may practice the evening before the speech or perhaps an hour before the actual presentation. Follow the speaker the day before in order to determine when he's going to practice. By preparing in advance, you can identify the frequencies and have them programmed into your scanner before the meeting begins.

(3) **Establish a temporary listening post.** If you can't pick up the signal in your room, establish a temporary listening post in a restroom stall near the auditorium. Restrooms are always located adjacent to auditoriums for the convenience of attendees. You'll have no trouble

finding an open stall once the meeting begins; with battery-powered equipment, you can wait, listen, and record in silence.

If you cannot pick up the signal in your hotel room, establish a temporary listening post in a restroom stall.

EXPERT TIP: Always use fresh batteries, and change them daily, regardless of how little or how long they were used the day before.

(4) **Find out if there will be multiple speakers.** The audio techs often have different microphone transmitters for each guest. The transmitters are controlled to prevent any frequency drift. As you pick up different speakers, take note of the frequencies being used. These will remain the same throughout the presentation (and, possibly, the convention).

(5) **Tape it.** Connect a small, portable tape recorder to the output of the scanner, and you'll have a perfect record of what was said.

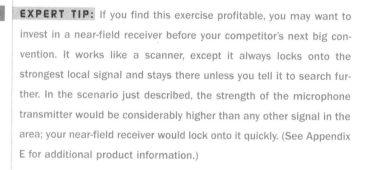

EXPERT TIP: If you find this exercise profitable, you may want to invest in a near-field receiver before your competitor's next big convention. It works like a scanner, except it always locks onto the strongest local signal and stays there unless you tell it to search further. In the scenario just described, the strength of the microphone transmitter would be considerably higher than any other signal in the area; your near-field receiver would lock onto it quickly. (See Appendix E for additional product information.)

SEARCHING A COMPETITOR'S HOME, OFFICE, OR HOTEL ROOM

Sometimes the company secret you need won't be found discarded in the trash or sitting unguarded on a meeting table. Sometimes it will be locked away in an executive's home, office, or hotel room. And here's where things get a little dark. Literally.

During World War II, these search operations were called "surreptitious entries." During the Cold War, such activities became known as "black-bag jobs"—the name derived from the small black bag of lock tools carried by the entry specialist. In Canada, the RCMP Security Service called them "Operation 300s." The code names vary by country, but the structure and techniques employed are generally the same. In an ideal situation, you'll want to assemble a four-person team made up of the following individuals:

The *lookout* is positioned at the observation post, monitoring radio frequencies to determine if an unseen alarm has been triggered. He or she maintains constant contact with the entry team and alerts them to unanticipated visits by security workers, residents, and so on.

The *lock specialist* is responsible for overcoming all interior locks or physical barriers that were not identified before the entry. After the entry has been achieved and any barriers overcome, the lock specialist supports the efforts of the search specialist.

The *photographer* takes numerous Polaroid photos of all areas to be searched before anything is touched. Depending on the size of the target and areas to be searched, it's not uncommon to take 100 or more photographs. The photographer coordinates the copying of documents that may be identified during the search. The photographer is also responsible for restoring the appearance of searched areas to be consistent with the initial Polaroids taken upon entry.

The *search specialist*'s job depends on the type of target. If the target is a computer, the specialist will have the required skills to access a hard drive, determine passwords, plant special monitoring software in the computer, and so on. If the target is not a computer, the search specialist will be familiar with the techniques needed to search a room (see Section B10).

Warning: Before you go hiring your own personal A-team, keep something in mind: This is highly illegal. These are exactly the same kinds of shenanigans that took down Richard Nixon back in 1974 and disillusioned Americans everywhere. Our attorneys have asked us to remind you that the following instructions are for entertainment only. Okay? Okay.

(1) **Consider every other option.** Ensure that other options for retrieving the information have been explored, and no practical alternatives exist for gathering the information.

(2) **Have specific goals.** The more intrusive your search, the longer it takes to restore order to the premises to cover your activities. Knowing exactly what you are going after will save you time and effort.

(3) **Thoroughly case the target in advance of an entry.** Get to know the building layout, entry and exit routes, exterior locks, primary and secondary escape routes, security systems, interior locks and physical barriers, and work patterns of staff and/or residents.

(4) **Bring duplicate keys.** Locks are difficult to pick, and the time necessary to manipulate a specific lock can be unpredictable. Only under the most extraordinary circumstances should an entry operation go forward without first obtaining copies of the original keys (see Section A1). Given enough time and planning, the original keys can usually be obtained by bribery, theft, or sleight of hand.

(5) **Dress appropriately.** All team members must wear clear latex gloves that maintain dexterity but eliminate fingerprints. If interior cameras record activities after hours, quick-on and -off facial disguises should be worn. Whatever the team wears, make sure a cover story is ready in case trouble develops, and the operation must be aborted.

(6) **Get in, and get out.** The longer you remain on the premises, the greater your chance of being caught or exposed. Search the most likely areas first. It makes no sense to search beneath the carpet if the object of the search is a computer hard drive.

(7) **Cover your tracks.** For maximum effect, the target should never realize that an entry took place. Everything brought in for the search should be removed at the conclusion; nothing should be left behind. Smoking is not permitted; food or beverages are not to be consumed during the entry or search operation. Remember: Getting caught is not an option. Just ask E. Howard Hunt.

C9

READING A COMPETITOR'S LAPTOP

Overworked executives often use the time spent on airplanes to prepare highly sensitive briefing papers, presentations, and meeting notes on their laptop computers. They'd be better off hitting the drink cart—especially if a spy who knows the following tricks happens to be aboard.

(1) **Fly first-class or business class.** This will give you the greatest access to business intelligence. Sure, people flying coach do work on their laptops—but the clubby atmosphere at the front of the plane is more relaxed, and executives there may feel more comfortable talking shop.

(2) **Schedule your flight accordingly.** Morning flights are better for obtaining information in advance of meetings, and late-afternoon flights are best for listening in on conversations about meetings just completed.

(3) **Choose your seat carefully.** To some extent, you're at the mercy of the airline reservation system—but you can often move to a vacant seat as soon as the door to the plane is closed, just before the aircraft pushes off to begin taxiing. A single business traveler is likely to work on a laptop, while two individuals together will probably review a presentation or debrief each other on the day's meetings. If your target is flying solo, sit beside him or her. If your target has a companion, sit directly behind them.

(4) **Close one eye.** To observe a fellow traveler's laptop or notes discreetly, utilize this old magician's trick. Pretend to be asleep, with your seat fully reclined. Your head should be slightly turned toward your fellow passenger. Close the eye that is closer to your target. Your open eye is blocked from the target's vision by the bridge of your nose. A little practice and experimentation will help you develop a body position that provides both comfort and covert observation.

Pretend to be asleep, and your neighbor won't realize you're monitoring him.

(5) **Take notes.** If you're sitting in the row behind your targets, it will be easy to jot down notes on your laptop as they talk—everyone will assume you're absorbed in your own work. If you're sitting next to your target, read his or her work carefully, and remember as much as possible; when the target takes a nap or starts reading the latest Michael Crichton book, go to the bathroom to jot down your notes before you forget the information.

CIO

USING YOUR CELL PHONE AS A NEGOTIATION TOOL

Every negotiation is a type of dance: the buyer wants to pay as little as possible, and the seller wants to gain as much as possible. The buyer subtly implies that the price of the item should be reduced, while the seller subtly implies that the price should be raised. Somewhere, amid all of the fancy footwork, is the bottom line. Forget the Arthur Murray crap, and use this spy trick to cut to the chase in your next meeting.

(1) **Obtain two cell phones.** Borrow one from a friend. While you have that friend available, ask for another favor. . . .

(2) **Place your friend in a comfortable, quiet spot with access to a third phone.**

(3) **Prepare the phones.** Before the meeting, turn on your cell phone (cell 1). Put it in silent mode, then call your friend. Keep the line open. Take the other cell phone (cell 2) and hide it in your jacket pocket. Make sure it is turned off.

(4) **Enter the meeting.** As you enter the conference room, place cell 1 facedown on the table adjacent to your briefcase. It is transmitting every word of the negotiation to your confederate.

(5) **Cut to the chase.** After consuming several cups of coffee, announce to your opponent that you need to visit the restroom. On your way out,

say, "Look, we're all professionals and understand what is going on in these negotiations. Let's save ourselves some time and get down to business." Ask them to think of the best possible price they are willing to accept, and say you'll conclude the negotiation when you return. When you split for the lavatory, leave all of your materials, including cell 1, in place. Now, turn on cell 2 in the privacy of the restroom stall.

(6) **Take your time.** As soon as you've gone, your opponents will discuss the price—they don't want to be trapped in the room any longer than you do. They'll decide on two prices: their optimum price and the minimum they'll accept.

(7) **Wait for your friend to call you on cell 2.** As soon as your friend hears the magic numbers, he or she will hang up on cell 1 and call you with the skinny.

(8) **Return to the meeting.** Armed with these numbers, return to the meeting and make your offer, shooting high or low, depending on the situation. Then proceed to "compromise" until you've reached the number that was heard by your confederate. Never go straight to their minimum or maximum price.

EXPERT TIP: To be certain that this technique will work, first visit the premises and verify that an adequate signal is attainable both inside the conference room and in the restroom stall by both cell phones. If the signal is weak, try to arrange the meeting at a location with better coverage.

SECTION D
TRANSMITTING SENSITIVE INFORMATION

01

MAKING UNTRACEABLE PHONE CALLS

In business, it is sometimes necessary to call someone and be sure that they don't have the ability to trace your phone call. Unfortunately, the telephone company—not to mention anyone who has caller ID—can trace all standard phone calls. If you want to make a completely anonymous, untraceable call, head to your nearest convenience store, where you can purchase the perfect device.

Head to your local convenience store for everything you need to make discreet, untraceable phone calls.

(1) **Purchase a prepaid calling card.** These are credit-card-sized, brightly colored, and displayed behind the counter in most convenience stores. Most offer inexpensive, high-quality calling anywhere in the United States—and sometimes throughout the world. These cards are made available by bulk purchasers of communications airtime who buy minutes in quantity and sell them at what appears to be an unbelievable bargain. If you are making the purchase to save money, think again—there are usually numerous hidden service charges and fees. But for maintaining privacy, these suckers can't be beat.

(2) **Dial the toll-free number on the back of the card.** You can do it from any pay phone—and from that moment on, your call is virtually untraceable. The calls show up as coming from "out of area," even if you're calling from across the street. Your call is buried in a sea of discount calls that are being placed by a variety of carriers in the United States and abroad. Spies, cheating spouses, blackmailers, and obscene callers use these cards all the time. Note that it is preferable to initiate the call from a pay phone, since your home-phone records could be checked or subpoenaed later.

D2

SENDING ANONYMOUS E-MAILS

Every time you send an e-mail, an electronic trail is created. The e-mail that shows up in someone's in-box displays fairly generic information— your e-mail address, time, date, addressee, and subject. There is, however, more detailed information in the Internet header, which can be accessed using your e-mail software.

Most people who send anonymous e-mails will use one of the following two methods—both of which have serious weaknesses.

Bad Idea 1: Creating a "disposable" e-mail account using Hotmail or another open-source e-mail account available to anyone—and then sending the e-mail from a public-access terminal at a public library, Internet café, or copy shop.

The Problem: Even these disposable accounts can be traced back to the source computer, and there may be video surveillance cameras monitoring public-access Internet terminals. Al Qaeda operatives involved in the September 11, 2001, attacks used this technique to communicate from Internet cafés throughout Europe—and they were discovered. As a result, any public-access site can be considered a prime target for cyber-surveillance.

Bad Idea 2: Sending the e-mail through an "anonymous" Web server (usually located abroad) that strips the identifying Internet header information from your e-mail so that it can't be tracked back to you.

The Problem: Even though the e-mail reaches its destination without the Internet header information, there is a record on the anonymous site's computers of your initial e-mail. Any e-mails from you to the anonymous site could be monitored, particularly if you're tangling with powerful forces.

To send an anonymous e-mail that *really* can't be traced back to you, follow these steps:

(1) **Obtain a promotional AOL CD-ROM.** Make sure it allows you to open a trial e-mail account without a credit card. AOL distributes these CD-ROMs by the millions, in the hopes that, after the free trial period, you'll become a subscriber. Since the account can be opened by virtually anyone, you will appear to the AOL computer as anyone you purport to be. These CD-ROMs are available free of charge at bookstores, at office-supply superstores, and with a pound of pressed ham at most neighborhood delicatessens.

(2) **Make an anonymous telephone call to AOL with a prepaid calling card.** Use this technique to dial AOL from your computer to establish your new account. By using your prepaid toll-free calling card, you are establishing the new account without any link to your real identity or home telephone number. Even the number that you're dialing AOL from can be in a different part of the country, since you're using the prepaid calling card and a toll-free number.

(3) **Establish a Hotmail account.** List your new AOL address as your home account. Do not choose a Hotmail screen name that hints at your own name or profession. Opt for a random sequence of letters and numbers, or a name intended to cause confusion, such as competitor@hotmail.com.

(4) **Send the anonymous e-mail from the new Hotmail account.** Remember, you must be logged on to AOL through your prepaid calling card so that nothing in the entire process can be traced back to you.

(5) **Destroy all evidence.** Remember that the hard drive in your computer will retain a copy of the original e-mail message. To be certain that the e-mail remains anonymous, remove your hard drive and physically destroy it. (This can be an expensive way to send one anonymous e-mail—so make it a good one.)

EXPERT TIP: There's a free e-mail encryption program called PGP (Pretty Good Privacy) that allows you to communicate with another person via e-mail without fear of third-party interception. You can download it from www.pgpi.org. Is it effective? Let's put it this way: Terrorist Ramzi Yousef—who bombed the World Trade Center in 1993—used PGP to protect his laptop files. When police discovered his laptop in 1995, it took the code-breaking resources of the National Security Agency more than 12 months to break through the encryption that was protecting his files.

D3

SENDING ANONYMOUS FAXES

Sometimes an anonymous phone call or e-mail simply won't cut the mustard, and a fax transmission is your only option. You may need to send a tip to the media about a competitor, a note to the boss about a competitor for a promotion, or even a whistle-blowing tip to the regulatory authorities.

In each of these cases, a fax traced back to you could spell disaster if:

A. The telltale tag line on the fax identifies your sending number.

B. The call can be traced back to the sender (i.e., you).

C. Distinguishing characteristics on the face of the fax identify you.

You can eliminate these problems by using the following techniques.

(1) **Change the tag line.** Locate the instruction manual for the fax machine, and find the section about entering the fax number that is printed on transmissions. Remove your identifying fax number and enter a fictional fax number—or perhaps the number of a competitor or colleague you would like to have identified as the originator of the fax. After making the change, send a test fax to another fax machine you control to verify the printout.

(2) **Use a prepaid calling card (see Section D1) to dial the destination fax machine.** As soon as you hear the fax tone, press the SEND button on your fax machine to begin to transmit manually. The display on your fax machine will provide visual confirmation that the fax is connecting.

(3)   **Cover your tracks.** The fax should contain no clues about your identity, so avoid handwritten notes. To cause additional mischief, send the fax using the letterhead of a competitor. The form can be salvaged from a fax you've received previously and doctored to restore it to its original, pristine condition.

(4)   **Destroy the fax confirmation receipt.**

(5)   **Restore the original tag line of your fax machine.** Send another fax to a controlled fax number, using conventional procedures, to verify that the machine has been restored to its original configuration.

(6)   **Clear the machine's databank.** Some fax machines keep a record of the last ten fax numbers dialed; send at least ten bogus faxes to clear the memory. Alternatively, search the fax machine manual for instructions on resetting the memory.

D4

PROTECTING YOUR CONVERSATIONS

During the Cold War, the RCMP Security Service needed an inexpensive, low-tech method to stop Soviet spies from overhearing key conversations while in Canada. They knew that traditional methods of sound masking—turning up the TV volume or running a shower—were highly ineffective. Audio techs could filter out the masking noise and uncover the conversation beneath.

The solution came when Canadian eavesdroppers noted how difficult it was to distinguish the speech of a targeted diplomat from that of nearby conversations at a foreign embassy cocktail party. If you didn't have a sufficient number of microphones hidden in the room, and the tonal quality and accents of the recorded voices were similar, the sounds picked up would be too jumbled to be comprehensible. From this observation, they developed the "jabber tape" (also known as a cocktail tape), a simple, inexpensive sound-masking technique that works as well today as it did in the 1970s.

The idea is to flood the conversation area—your hotel room, office, conference room, or automobile—with a jumble of sounds and words from a tape recorder that plays while you have your secret conversation. Your secrets will be protected from eavesdroppers, since the recorded jabber cannot be separated or removed by electronic filtering.

If you're afraid that someone is recording your conversations—or, worse, perched outside your office with a drinking glass pressed against the door—here's what to do.

(1) **Prepare your small microcassette recorder, and begin to speak into the microphone.** Open a book to a random page (we recommend any of the fine titles from Quirk Books, available for order at www.quirkbooks.com). Beginning with the last word on the page, read every third word aloud, going backward up the page. Speak in a normal conversational tone—not too fast, not too slow. Proceed for a full hour to fill the tape. (And make sure no one's listening to you do this, or they'll call a priest.) This is Tape 1.

(2) **Prepare a second microcassette recorder with a new tape.** Play Tape 1 several feet away from your microphone. Ask an associate to read aloud from a different book, using the same technique described in Step 1. The microphone on your tape recorder will record your friend's voice as well as the jabber playing from Tape 1.

(3) **Continue this process as many times as you like, with at least two or three voices of the same gender and general tone.** (In other words, don't make a jabber tape with Joan Rivers, Ice-T, and a Scottish bartender.) Just remember that the final version of your tape should not just be a jumble of noise, but a stream of meaningless words being spoken distinctly at various volume levels.

(4) **Finally, save your tape, and employ it whenever you suspect someone might be listening.** For the technique to work as an effective sound mask, the volume of the jabber tape should be at least twice the volume of the actual secret conversation. The audio speakers playing the jabber tape should be located as close to you as possible.

HEART MONTH NEVER HOPING MEET SET FOOD DIRECTIONS YOU COUNT WARM ME ANGRY GROWS RIDDLE PATCHES MATTERS GETS WIND PREPACK MANY STICK HOWLING COCKTAIL TONIGHT STARES NOTE INTO YES CASTLE AT SISTER COULDN'T LAKE REALLY YES SOUTH WHIRL ARMY THIS BEST EIGHTY-ONE FOUR STOPPING FALLS UNTIL MESSAGE THIRTY ACTIONS INDEX WASN'T DISTURB AGENT

Use a "jabber tape" to prevent enemy spies from overhearing your most secret conversations.

05

EMBEDDING SECRET MESSAGES IN COMPUTER FILES

PowerPoint, the über-popular presentation software, is all about show-ing off your precious research and creative ideas. It also happens to be a great place to hide all of your most valued secrets.

The technique is called "corporate microdots," and it allows you to conceal information inside an ordinary PowerPoint presentation. The beauty is that there is no separate reference to the file on your com-puter's hard drive; if anyone should open and examine the file, he or she would only see a standard presentation. And unless somebody knows the specific slide number and the precise location of the microdot hid-den on the page, it will remain hidden. Here's how it works.

(1) **Open an existing PowerPoint presentation.** Or, alternatively, create a new one.

(2) **Create a new slide.** Go to *Insert* on the tool bar, open the pull-down menu, and select *New Slide* to create the slide for the hidden microdot.

(3) **Choose a color.** Either stay with the background color that the new slide opens with, or go to the tool bar, select *Format,* and then select *Background* to change the color. Let's assume you've selected white as your background color.

(4) **Add your message.** Select either of the text boxes that appear with a new slide, and type in the text you want to hide. The message can be as long as you want. You could retype a Tom Clancy novel in a PowerPoint text box.

(5) **Change the text color.** After you've completed your message, select and highlight all of the text. Go to the tool bar, and change the color of the font to the same color as the background of your slide (in this case, white).

(6) **Deselect the highlighted text.** Your message will become invisible. Of course, the text is still there, but you can't see it because it is the same color as the background.

(7) **Shrink the box.** Click on any of the four corner handles of the text box, and drag it diagonally to reduce the box to its smallest size.

(8) **Make the box disappear.** After you've reduced the box as much as possible (there is a built-in limit), click the outline of the text box, and drag it anywhere on the page. To place it in a specific location that is known only to you, first go to the tool bar and click on *View,* then *Grid and Guides.* Ensure that *Display grid on screen* is checked, and then click *OK*. With the grid visible, you can drag your microdot to any of the resulting boxes created by the grid. If you chart the grid boxes beginning in the upper left and count from left to right, you'll have a way to remember, or tell someone else, where the microdot is hidden. When you deselect the box and turn off the grid lines, it becomes invisible. Congratulations, you've just created a corporate microdot.

(9) **Add one additional level of security.** To obscure the microdot further, insert an image or graphic into your slide, and paste it over the invisible microdot. Spies during World War II would frequently paste a postage stamp over a microdot being mailed out on an envelope. (See "Spies at Work," opposite.)

(10) **To recover and read your microdot, follow these simple instructions.**

A. Turn on the grid to enable location of the microdot.

B. Move any image that may be covering the microdot.

C. Select the microdot.

D. Click one of the corner handles and drag outward to enlarge the image.

E. Highlight the text (it becomes temporarily visible while highlighted).

F. Change the color of the font for it to remain visible.

G. Read, copy, or print out the slide containing the concealed text.

SPIES AT WORK

During World War II and the Cold War, spies used a technique of secret writing called "microdots" to communicate with their officers. These dots were effective tools because they contained a full page of text and could be concealed (or buried) in a postcard, envelope, or letter. The dot, containing a condensed, photographed page of text, was not much larger than the period at the end of this sentence. To read a dot, it was necessary to place it under a microscope or in an optical viewer that would enlarge the text. Dots were further camouflaged by diluted iodine, which acted like bleach and made the dots practically invisible.

Of course, microdots were extraordinarily difficult to produce—and reading them required optical equipment and a darkroom, two things most field agents lack. But during the Cold War, Lucien Nikolai, the director of clandestine photography for the KGB, developed a microdot system that required only a 35 mm camera with a high-quality lens. He even developed a way for the spy in the field to produce the necessary microdot film using only vodka, headache medicine, the clear cellophane wrapping from a cigarette pack, and a few other household chemicals. The KGB and the GRU (Soviet military intelligence) utilized this technique as their primary method for communicating with agents during much of the Cold War.

06

COMMUNICATING SECRETLY WITH CO-WORKERS

Some bosses love to take walks around the office to observe the staff at random times. This can be very annoying, especially when you're trying to run clandestine operations. To prevent unexpected surprises, it's useful to have a code that you and your colleagues can use to sound the alert when the boss (code-named Big Dog) is on the prowl.

The solution comes from U.S. POWs who were trapped in Vietnam. Prisoners were forbidden to talk with each other, but they were desperate to find a way to communicate secretly. One of the officers remembered an old World War II prisoner's code that used taps instead of the dots and dashes of Morse code. (This was necessary since the prisoners had no way to send dashes when tapping on the prison walls.) The tap code was based on a five-by-five matrix. Each letter was communicated by tapping two numbers; the first number was for the row, the second number for the column.

To fit the alphabet into the 25 spaces in the five-by-five matrix, the letter K was eliminated and replaced by C during transmissions (so the word look would be communicated as looc).

	1	2	3	4	5
1	A	B	C	D	E
2	F	G	H	I	J
3	L	M	N	O	P
4	Q	R	S	T	U
5	V	W	X	Y	Z

For example, the letter *W* would be communicated as "5 (pause) 2." *I* would be sent as "2 (pause) 4." The letter *X* was used to break up sentences. Once, after North Vietnamese captors played some Joan Baez antiwar songs over the prison camp's public address system, a message was transmitted among prisoners using this code. The message: "Joan Baez succs."

In the office, a handy acronym would be *BDA* (for Big Dog Alert). Using the POW tap code, it would sound like 1–2, 1–4, 1–1. To make sure everyone hears, tap your heavy college ring against a ceramic mug. It will make a distinct noise that can be heard throughout the office. When Big Dog leaves for the day or returns to his office, send out the signal 1–1, 1–3, or *AC* for All Clear.

2–3, 1–1, 3–5, 3–5, 5–4, 4–4, 1–1, 3–5, 3–5, 2–4, 3–3, 2–2!

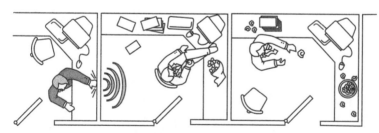

Employ the secret codes of U.S. POWs in cubicles of all different shapes and sizes to communicate secretly upon the boss's arrival.

SPIES AT WORK

The tap code was later modified by U.S. Navy rear admiral Jeremiah Denton, who was shot down on July 18, 1965, and released by the North Vietnamese government on February 12, 1973. He developed a verbal version of the tap code that could be used by shackled prisoners who couldn't tap. He employed "cough," "sniff," "clear throat," "hack," and "sneeze" to indicate rows and columns 1 through 5. A prisoner recalled that the first time he heard the vocal tap code, he thought he had been placed in the tuberculosis ward.

VOCAL TAP CODE

	Cough	Sniff	Clear Throat	Hack	Sneeze
Cough	A	B	C	D	E
Sniff	F	G	H	I	J
Clear Throat	L	M	N	O	P
Hack	Q	R	S	T	U
Sneeze	V	W	X	Y	Z

07

COMMUNICATING WITH INVISIBLE INKS

Secret writing systems have been used for hundreds of years. The most practical systems have two components: the ink used to write the message and the reagent needed to recover it.

Most kinds of paper can hide secret writing, but experiment with different types to determine which works best with your method of choice. You can use secret writing on the last page of a deposit slip in a checkbook, the endpapers of a favorite novel, or even the paper backing on a framed photo. You can also write secret messages on the margins of letters and postcards, or on the inside of an envelope. Once it is encrypted and hidden, only you (and your trusted contact) will be able to read the message.

The following "inks" are available in or near any office building.

(1) **Eyedrops.** Carry a small bottle of eyedrops designed to relieve red eyes. Dip a cotton swab into the solution, then write your message. Allow it to air-dry until the words become invisible. To read the message, hold it under a black light. The writing will remain invisible for years to come.

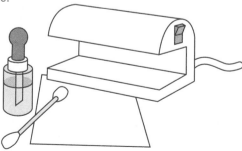

(2) **Baking soda.** Mix a tablespoon of baking soda and a tablespoon of water. Dip a cotton swab into the solution, then write your message. Allow it to air-dry—you can use a blow-dryer to speed up the process. To read the message, dribble purple grape juice over the message. After doing this, the message will remain visible.

(3) **Laxative tablets.** Purchase a laxative pill that contains phenolph-thalein (Ex-Lax, for example). Open or crush the pill into a small cup, then add one tablespoon of rubbing alcohol. Dip a cotton swab into the solution, then write your message. Allow it to air-dry. To read the message, spray it with an ammonia-based glass cleaner; the writing will turn pink and remain visible.

(4) **Urine.** It's best not to try this one at your desk. Dilute the urine with tap water until it's clear. Dip a cotton swab in the urine, then write your message (don't use too much of the solution, or the paper will buckle). Allow the message to air-dry. To read the message, aim a hot blow-dryer at it or expose it to the heat of a light bulb, held just below the paper. The message will appear and remain visible.

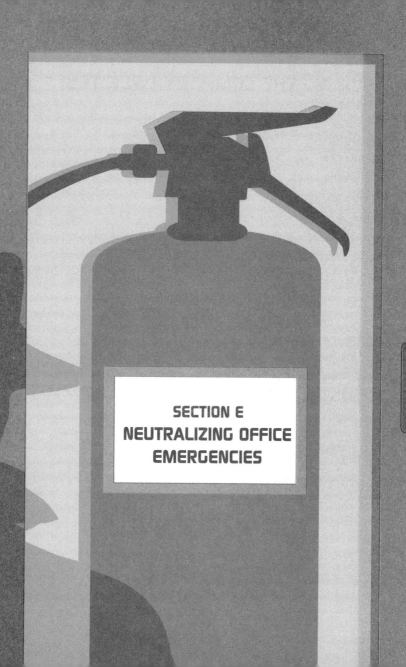

SECTION E
NEUTRALIZING OFFICE
EMERGENCIES

PASSING THE COMPANY DRUG TEST

East German athletes—that phrase alone should be enough to give you pause—developed a unique technique for passing announced drug tests that was both ingenious and shocking.

By the 1980s, drug testing had evolved, and most of the known techniques for cheating had been eliminated. Once an athlete had taken any performance-enhancing drugs, it was no longer possible to mask the urine without detection. The only remaining option was to find a way of substituting clean urine for tainted urine. To prevent this, the athlete's urine had to be deposited in a sampling cup that registered the temperature of the liquid. If the temperature was anything other than the athlete's own body temperature, it was not accepted, and the athlete was disqualified.

The technique seemed impossible to defeat. But a few athletes were able to beat the test with advice from the Stasi, East Germany's internal security service. If you find yourself in desperate—and we mean desperate—need of passing a company drug test, you might find the following technique useful.

(1) **Obtain clean urine.** Find someone who doesn't own any black lights, bongs, or Phish albums. Ask him or her to donate a sample of urine for the greater good. (Your greater good, to be precise.)

(2) **Heat it up.** The greatest challenge in beating a high-tech drug test, of course, is having the urine's temperature match your body's. Maybe your company doesn't worry about taking the temperature of

your sample, but if it does, follow the example of the East Germans, who inserted small rubber balloons into their rectums and pumped it full of four ounces of clean urine. Once inserted, there was no external indication of the device, other than a small, clear plastic tube that began at the anus and terminated behind the testicles, where it was held in place by a small piece of adhesive.

3 **Deliver the specimen when asked.** When it became time for the East German athlete to provide the sample, he would turn away from the testers and pull slightly on the tube. This motion released a small plastic valve inside the balloon, and the clean urine—at his exact body temperature—flowed into the cup.

With practice, the technique can be completed in one smooth motion that appears and sounds like the natural expulsion of urine from the body. Female athletes used the same technique; the vaginal orifice made concealment of the apparatus even easier and slightly more comfortable for the athlete.

Turn your back to the testers when providing a sample to afford yourself the opportunity to utilize the clean urine you've prepared.

CONSTRUCTING A PHONE ALIBI TAPE

When your boss mistakenly assumes you're diligently taking notes at a regional meeting, a believable alibi can rescue you from an otherwise risky situation. When you place a telephone call, the recipient has only three ways to judge the veracity of where you say you are: caller ID, which identifies the originating telephone number; information you volunteer about your location; and ambient background noises that give clues to your whereabouts.

To deal with caller ID, either block the identifying information from your telephone or make an untraceable call using a pre-paid calling card (see Section D1). In many cases, it may be appropriate to call from your cell phone, even if you are supposed to be in another part of the country. (After all, the originating number will always be yours.)

Now you simply need to provide credible information and a few background noises to back up your story. To deal with the latter, you can create and employ an *alibi tape*.

(I) **Record various sounds.** It helps to have a variety on file: office chatter, cocktail-lounge murmurs, street noise, and so on. The following four sounds are especially persuasive:

A. Airport-lounge noise, such as boarding announcements, departures being called for different cities, and so on. If your boss thinks you're leaving for a business trip abroad, visit the airport ahead of time to collect a recording of the flight being called.

B. The flight attendant's announcement to "Please discontinue use of cellular telephones, and buckle your seat belts" prior to takeoff. (This provides a great excuse for ending the call, as well.)

C. The distinctive foreign voice of an overseas telephone operator announcing, "Please hold for an international call." The voice never says who is calling, or from where, but you can provide that missing information.

D. Hospital waiting-room announcements. This one is particularly handy if you suddenly "fall ill" and cannot attend an important meeting.

(2) **Record at least five minutes of each separate background noise.** On a 60-minute cassette, you can conveniently store 11 different background sounds. Leave at least 30 seconds of empty tape between each different background sound—to prevent mysterious tugboat sounds when your boss believes you are stranded in an airport.

(3) **Practice, practice, practice.** Hold the tape recorder at various distances away from the telephone mouthpiece; experiment with various volume levels. Dial your voice-mail account and leave messages using a variety of techniques. Later, play back the messages and see how believable your recorded background noise sounds. Adjust accordingly until you feel confident enough to make the real call.

E3

CALLING IN SICK

The sounds of illness can be faked in a number of ways. The recipient of the call has very little to go on other than your work record, your position in the company, your cover story, and your hideous hacking or sneezing.

(1) **Have your spouse call in sick for you.** This is an old standby, so most people are wise to the trick. This technique generally only works if you have a spotless work record or if you have a known illness or recent injury. For instance, if you were seen the day before falling off a file cabinet while changing a lightbulb, everyone will understand your absence the next day.

(2) **Construct an alibi tape.** The next time you really are sick with a bad cold or the flu, take some steps to obtain some unscheduled time off in the future. Construct your alibi tape (see Section E2) by recording a few phrases:

"This is April . . . I've come down . . . [sneeze] . . . with the flu and will be out at least through tomorrow. As soon as my . . . [cough, cough] fever comes down, I'll be in."

"This is April . . . [sneeze] . . . please cancel all my appointments for today. I'll . . . [cough, cough] . . . try to come in tomorrow, but this feels like a 48-hour bug."

In the future, when you need to take a day off, just call the office before anyone arrives. Hold the tape recorder up to the telephone, and play one of these tracks. Because you are leaving a message, you don't have to worry about answering additional questions, and since you made the tape when you really were sick, it will sound convincing. When the rest of the gang arrives at work, they'll find your message and lament your suffering. (These alibi tapes are timeless, unless you overuse them.)

3. **Employ extreme measures.** If you've already called in sick several times and need a real whopper of an excuse, try this method. Call the office to report your illness or accident using your cell phone. As you are providing the report of your plight, play your alibi tape of hospital noises in the background. You might include a female voice that barks, "Sir, you'll have to turn off that cell phone—it interferes with the hospital equipment!" In a hushed voice, tell your office, "I'm feeling terrible. I've got to go, but I'll call after the doctor arrives and gives me something for the pain."

Don't answer your cell phone for the rest of the day. The office can't call the hospital to ask about your condition, because you never identified the hospital in the first place. Enjoy a day of golfing, then call the next day to explain that the medicine made you so groggy you forgot to check in.

E4

APPEARING INJURED

Instead of calling in sick, you might try the ol' bodily injury trick. But you can't bounce into the office the next day with a fresh suntan and a serene, relaxed look on your face. First, you need to get your mental game straight. Don't complain excessively—let the physical effects of your injury confirm the obvious. Explaining what happened in too much detail is usually worse than not saying enough.

Now, on to the physical game. Faking a cast is overkill; plus, you'll be stuck with it for weeks. Better to stick with soft-tissue injuries, such as a sprained ligament or pulled tendon. These require wrapping and isolation of the injured area, plus the use of a cane, sling, or crutches. Any of these three props are terrific, since they provide visible confirmation of your injury. Plus, these kinds of injuries often heal within a few days.

(I) **Wrap a bandage around the affected joint.** This limits the joint's motion and alters the way you stand and walk. A little hobbling when you arrive will demonstrate the injury. This is easy to fake but also easy to forget as the day continues. Here's how to keep up the act.

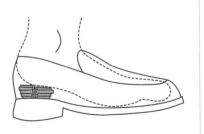

A. For an ankle or leg injury, place several layers of thick cardboard inside the heel of one shoe. Wedge a thumbtack between the layers so that its tip protrudes slightly. The faint, nagging pain will be a constant reminder of your injury.

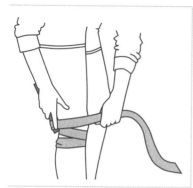

B. For a knee injury, place a semi-flexible metal ruler against the back of your knee and wrap it in place with a bandage. This will make a noticeable difference in the way you stand and walk.

C. For a back injury, purchase an elastic shoulder brace from a medical supply store. Used correctly, it will pull both shoulders back and help with posture. However, worn backward, it has the opposite effect and will pull your shoulders forward into a decided stoop. You can probably feel the sympathy from your colleagues already.

(2) **Don't forget the physical therapy.** If the weather is good, don't forget to head outside every day to work on your handicap. If you need additional proof that you're receiving therapeutic treatment, create a track for your alibi tape with the sound of a whirlpool running in the background. Play it when you check in with the office before beginning your "treatment" (i.e., teeing off).

SPIES AT WORK

During World War II, the British military's intelligence service waged war by demoralizing the enemy. One of its successful techniques was to drop propaganda matchbooks on the German troops during the closing days of the war. (As the German economy faltered in 1945, matchbooks were considered prized possessions and were in short supply.) Each matchbook proclaimed that the war was lost and urged the soldier reading the matchbook not to be the last one to die in "Hitler's war." The matchbook instructed the soldier to feign illness and go to the hospital. Detailed instructions told the soldier the necessary steps for faking a real illness:

1 *"Take the powder from a rifle cartridge, and dissolve it in your daily mug of coffee. Do this each day until you begin to feel and look ill. Stop eating so that you will appear emaciated. Report to morning sick-call, and say you are too sick to fight. The doctor will make a preliminary diagnosis and send you to the hospital. You will return to good health in a week to ten days after you stop drinking the concoction. This will make you sick, but it's better than being dead."*

2 *"Rub black pepper in your eyes until they swell. Continue the action until your eyes are too swollen to see. Report to morning sick-call and explain that you can't see. Your sight will return; the pain and discomfort is better than the certain death that awaits you in combat."*

E5

LEAVING THE OFFICE UNDETECTED

Do you suspect that your boss has dispatched a minion to keep tabs on you during your lunch break? Follow this rule of thumb: If you see someone once during the day, it's interesting. If you see the person twice in a day, it's probably a coincidence. If you see the same person three times in the same day, it's likely that you are under active surveillance. Here's how to slip away from a watchful eye.

(1) **Always be aware of possible surveillance.** Note the people around you when you enter and depart your office, as well as throughout the day.

(2) **Alter your speed.** If you think you're being followed, act naturally. Then speed up or reduce your pace to see if the person is still there (see step 3); if so, you may be under surveillance.

(3) **Never look back.** Despite the way people behave in movies, you shouldn't be glancing constantly over your shoulder. If you want to take a look, use a store window or the reflection in the window of a parked car. If you're seen searching constantly for signs of surveillance, those interested in your activities (such as your boss) will devote *more* resources to tracking you, not less.

Another simple way to steal a glance behind you is called the "free look." Simply enter a store—a music store, a cheese shop, a corner café—and browse for a second, then change your mind and exit. Now, glance around as if you're deciding where to go next. Ah, that bakery across the way looks interesting. Jaywalk across the street, looking both ways as you cross. If you see one or more people jaywalking with you, you might be under surveillance.

(4) **Disguise yourself.** As you turn a corner, change as many visual indicators of your appearance as possible as you continue to walk. You'll be able to do this if you carry items in your briefcase or suspend them beneath your coat. Pack various styles of hats, a reversible jacket, a folding cane, glasses, or other items that alter your appearance. (For more ideas, see Section C3.)

(5) **Alter the direction of your travel.** Continue to walk at a brisk pace. If you still can't shake your tail, hop into a cab and return to the office. Pick another time to make a break for it. You can't be tailed forever.

E6

SURVIVING OFFICE IMPRISONMENT

Attending a long corporate meeting may feel like you're doing **time as a prisoner of war**. The proceedings are mind-numbing, the **pace monotonous**, the food distasteful—even by third world standards. A **prisoner of war** never loses the desire to escape, but still must face the **cruel reality** and learn to survive. Here's how the pros do it.

(1)   **Catch up on your reading.** Clip a recent article from *Rolling Stone* and photocopy it onto pages headed with the words *Quarterly Research Reports*. Using this technique, you can copy an unlimited number of interesting articles onto pages that will fit into a seminar binder. If the people sitting next to you notice you're busy reading the binder, they'll think you are either preparing for your own presentation or they'll obsess over the fact that they weren't important enough to receive binders of their own.

(2)   **Catch up on your writing.** Start writing a rough draft of your memoir, a great spy novel, or a letter to an old friend. It won't matter, since everyone else, including the presenter, will think that you're scribbling important meeting notes.

(3)   **Build or purchase something in your mind.** Popular subjects for hostages are:

A. Your dream house. Plan every element, including the site selection, home design, construction process (site work, foundation, plumbing,

SURVIVING OFFICE IMPRISONMENT

Always bring reading material to long meetings and sales presentations.

electrical, framing, Sheetrock, roof, furnishings, and yard with putting green), and, of course, the housewarming party.

B. Your dream car. Contrast different manufacturers, compare all models, select options and colors, and think about the first weekend trip to that vineyard you've always wanted to visit.

C. A piece of furniture you've always wanted to build—like a wet bar. Finish the design, select the wood, cut the pieces, sand each piece, perform the final fitting, and apply the exterior finish.

(4) **Maintain communication links with fellow captives.** This is essential for your sanity. By keeping in touch with others during the meeting, you'll pass the time and raise the spirits of another suffering human being. Consider these covert communication techniques:

A. Transmit infrared point-and-burst messages from your PDA (personal digital assistant) to co-workers' PDAs. It's a high-tech way to keep up on office gossip. Best of all, point-and-burst communications can't be intercepted or detected.

B. Go low-tech and pass notes. To avoid having your messages intercepted and read, write them in secret ink using the techniques detailed in Section D7.

On June 25, 1998, George Tenet, the director of the Central Intelligence Agency, presented the Director's Medal to CIA officers Dick Fecteau and Jack Downey for their amazing feats of heroism while held captive in China for more than 20 years.

In 1951, fresh from college, Fecteau and Downey joined the CIA. After a period of training, they were sent to East Asia to conduct agent resupply and pickup operations over China as part of the U.S. war effort in Korea. Fecteau and Downey dropped supplies and retrieved agents for debriefing by flying in low among the trees and literally snatching agents from the ground.

In November 1952, their plane was hit by gunfire. It crashed and burned, killing the two pilots. Fecteau and Downey survived, but they were captured by the forces of the People's Republic of China. Two years later, the Chinese government sentenced the men to life in prison. Over the next 20 years, the men were subjected to extensive and aggressive interrogations and long periods of solitary confinement.

Downey recalled their imprisonment and remembered being confined 23 hours a day to a 12-by-15-foot cell. He was terrified for the first few years, "But you learn to live with uncertainty and to stop feeling sorry for yourself. After all, if this is going to be the balance of your life, you have to make the best of it." He was allowed an hour a day in the small exercise yard, where he did chin-ups and jogged—44 laps to cover a mile. He received "a reasonable amount of food," the serving-size and quality varying according to the plenitude of China's harvest. He was neither beaten nor tortured and remained in good health.

Downey later remembered that maintaining mental alertness was one of the keys to survival. He never forgot his affiliation with the CIA or that he was an intelligence officer serving out a harsh post under an oppressive Chinese security bureau. He remembered that the best way to pass time was to "not think about it."

In December 1971, the United States finally obtained the release of Fecteau, and in March 1973, the release of Downey. Neither man let his experiences make him bitter; they reluctantly accepted their circumstances and were committed to surviving. When a reporter later asked Downey how he'd describe the 20 years he spent in prison, he answered, "They were a crashing bore! I won't dwell upon the past, because I'm too preoccupied with the present and the future."

TRANSFORMING A BRIEFCASE INTO A BULLETPROOF SHIELD

First of all, there is no such thing as bullet*proof*. The routine use of appropriate soft "bulletproof" body armor reduces the likelihood of fatal injury, but 100 percent protection in all circumstances is impossible. Body-armor selection is a tradeoff between protection and weight. The comfort of soft body armor is inversely proportional to the level of ballistic protection it provides.

The threat levels from pistols and rifles vary according to the type of ammunition, the weight of the projectile, and the velocity. Stopping a light projectile fired from a small-caliber handgun (.22) is vastly easier than stopping a bullet fired from a high-powered AK-47 assault rifle. To compare different levels of protection, the National Institute of Justice created an industry standard to measure the ballistic resistance of police body armor and to categorize armor by different levels.

Level I body armor is the minimum level of protection that you should have, and is totally suitable for full-time wear. Level II armor is worn full-time in some high-threat areas but may not be considered suitable for full-time use in hot, humid climates. Businessmen desiring more than minimum protection may consider wearing Level II-A armor, which has been found to be sufficiently comfortable for full-time concealable wear when the threat warrants it, and is lighter and less bulky than Level II. Level III and Level IV armor are very hard and heavy and are intended for use only in situations when the threat warrants extremely weighty protection. Level III-A armor, which provides the highest level of protection, is generally considered unsuitable for routine wear; however, individuals confronted with a terrorist threat may be willing to tolerate the weight and bulk of such armor.

Of course, any protective armor is worthless if you aren't wearing it when attacked—or when the clerk in accounts payable goes berserk. For that reason, consider adding armor plates inside your attaché case to create an emergency shield.

(1) **Obtain rigid armor plates.** Special armor plates constructed of polyethylene provide Level III protection. Composite plates combining both high-performance polyethylene and ceramic provide protection up to Level IV.

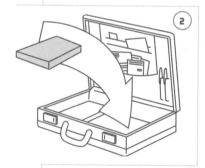

(2) **Attach the plates to the inside of your briefcase/attaché case with adhesive strips of Velcro.** Measuring 10 by 12 inches, these plates are classified as "stand alone" and can be inserted inside a standard briefcase to provide protection as an emergency shield. Two plates, side by side, will fit neatly on one side of a standard hard-shell attaché case. Even with Level IV protection, two plates add only a total of 14.4 pounds of weight (7.2 pounds each) but provide protection against a 30-06 rifle that is firing armor-piercing ammunition.

(3) **In the event of gunfire, hold the briefcase between the shooter and yourself at chest-level.** Pray for the best.

E8

DEALING WITH LETTER AND PACKAGE BOMBS

Letter and package bombs are continual hazards that are often cyclical and, unfortunately, subject to imitators. Whenever there are news reports about these devices anywhere in the world, there are subsequent copycat incidents. While frequently employed by terrorists, these devices are also used by ex-spouses and lovers who want to eliminate wives, husbands, rivals, and business associates. Security personnel should be alert for stalking, broken relationships, and threats of violence that may result in letter and package bombs.

Package bombs, including book bombs, are detonated by an electrical or mechanical system. In a letter bomb, the explosive is often wrapped around two pieces of cardboard with the detonator in between; the pressure of the envelope keeps the explosive from detonating. When the pressure is removed—as when someone pulls out the letter—the device explodes. A thorough examination of the envelope by the bomb squad will uncover the wires or detonator inside.

(1) **Never open any letter or package until you have inspected it.** If this rule is violated, all other information about bombs is useless.

(2) **Watch for warning signs.** If you fear that a letter or package is suspect, contact the police. To do otherwise risks lives and property damage. Few companies have adequate screening equipment, and the U.S. Postal Service does not x-ray all mail and packages. The following warning signs can alert you to potential problems:

A. The package is not expected.

B. The package or letter has been mailed from outside the country.

C. The purported sender is unknown to the recipient, or the style of the address appears nonstandard or contains spelling errors.

D. The package or letter uses some form of special delivery service such as certified or registered, or requires a personal signature upon delivery.

E. The package or letter is addressed only to a position such as "director" or "president," not to the specific person.

F. The package or letter has a strange smell—either pungent or almondlike.

G. The package or letter has oily stains.

Look out for excessive postage, oily stains, misspellings, uneven thickness, and an incomprehensible return address—all indicators of a package bomb.

H. The package or letter has excessive postage (to ensure that it is not returned).

I. The letter is $1/4$- to $1/2$-inch (0.6–1.3 cm) thick and in a rigid envelope.

J. The letter may be thicker at the top, bottom, or sides.

K. The letter has a greater weight than other letters of similar size.

L. You've angered someone in the recent past and have reason to be concerned.

(**3**) **Warn your co-workers.** While waiting for emergency personnel to arrive, calmly evacuate the building.

E9

ESCAPING FROM A HIGH-RISE BUILDING

As we all witnessed on September 11, 2001, working or living in a high-rise building carries risks. But a prepared and positioned escape kit enhances your chance of surviving a life-threatening disaster.

(1) **Prepare your escape plan and related equipment.** The plan should map out the exact route you will follow to escape from any floor. Know which stairwells descend completely and which extend only partially. Any locked doors that will impede your exit should be eliminated from consideration. Walk the escape route monthly so you are able to follow it in the event the building becomes smoke-filled. Be alert for any changes in building construction that may alter or limit your escape route. Continue to adjust and improve your escape plan.

(2) **Prepare your escape kit, including additional items as necessary.** Check your equipment and batteries every three months to ensure that they are intact and operational. Always have the following:

A. Swiss Army knife with multiple blades; a portable tool kit with numerous applications for escape.

B. Portable radio with spare batteries capable of tuning to AM radio stations for updated news. Ignore rumors at the site of the emergency.

c. Cell phone programmed with emergency numbers in speed dial. Even when conventional phone circuits are disabled, cellular is most likely to survive the disaster and remain in operation.

D. Flashlight with fresh batteries and bulbs, plus spares.

E. Smoke evac hood that offers an oxygen supply for 30 minutes (perfect for escaping smoke-filled corridors).

F. Portable first-aid kit to deal with emergency injuries. Delay all nonessential first aid until you have safely exited the building and the immediate area. Seek medical help away from the disaster.

G. Crowbar (small) for forcing locked doors and opening any blocked escape passages.

H. Map of building and alternative escape exits in case your primary escape route is blocked.

I. Comfortable footwear for rapid evacuation of the building. Excess clothing and footwear should be left behind.

3. **Keep your escape kit handy. It should be self-contained inside a nondescript medium backpack and located inside a desk drawer or cabinet.** Be prepared to grab it and depart within seconds. Don't brag or boast about your kit, but encourage others to prepare one of their own.

(4) **When a disaster happens, grab your kit and leave the area.** At worst you'll feel foolish if your escape was unnecessary. At best, it will save your life. When terrorism is concerned, there are no odd coincidences. If the situation appears unsafe or unusual, execute your escape.

APPENDICES

PADDING YOUR EXPENSE REPORT

Successful office spies need operating budgets—after all, you've got microcassette recorders, hats, canes, rubber tubes, and even armor plates to purchase. To hide your operating expenses within your actual business-related expenses—or simply to generate more money—try any or all of the following techniques.

1   **Be neat and on time.** Always submit legible, neatly prepared reports, and attach all required supporting documentation. The more you appear to adhere to company policies, the less likely your account will be singled out for additional audits or greater scrutiny.

2   **Never brag or reveal your expense-account secrets to others.** As soon as you do, you're vulnerable. Remember that today's good friend may be a future competitor for a promotion; if your "financial irregularities" ever come to light, you'll be eliminated from consideration. On a similar note, avoid taking tips from the office wise guy on how *he* pads *his* account. If he brags openly, he'll eventually be caught and his "foolproof" techniques exposed.

3   **Collect receipts.** As you shop or travel, always look for and collect cash receipts that people leave at or near the register. Maybe you had a bagel and coffee for breakfast ($2) but the person in front of you had the deluxe steak and eggs ($14). If that person leaves his receipt, take it and file it. (After all, you could have had the deluxe breakfast if you'd really wanted it.) Similarly, if you're going to the office-supply

store for presentation materials, pick up some extra receipts around the cash register. Everyone will remember the great presentation, not the extra $5 you allegedly spent on supplies.

4 **Be nice to cab drivers.** They'll give you an almost unlimited supply of blank receipts. Usually, when you ask for a receipt, they just hand you a blank. Fill it in as necessary, and keep the total reasonable. Whether you walk, take the subway, or catch a ride with someone else, you'll always have a supply of blank taxi receipts ready for documenting the cab ride you could have taken.

5 **Alter your receipts using a computer.** If your company allows the submission of photocopied receipts, you can re-create almost any type of legitimate receipt using graphic imaging programs such as Photoshop. Be sure you understand how to use the program before submitting a doctored receipt. Manipulated receipts are usually identifiable by:

A. **Variances in font.** The original receipt is printed in one font, but additions are in another.

B. **Smudged backgrounds involving security papers.** Some receipts are printed on security paper, which has an intricate pattern embedded in the background. The idea is to make it difficult for you to scan, copy, and paste different numbers onto the paper. Skillful use of the imaging software will allow you to overcome this problem, but not without extensive time and effort.

C. Layout Errors. Ensure that your work is neat and perfectly aligned. Many crude attempts at computer-aided manipulation are detected by uneven spacing or misalignment of the altered areas. If in doubt, measure the spaces between letters, words, and numbers. Your submitted version must be as clean and consistently spaced as the original.

D. Differences in color or clarity. Sometimes it is better to photocopy your manipulated receipt several times to give it the proper fuzzy and aged appearance of a real receipt. If you can detect a difference, an alert auditor will, too.

E. Mathematical errors. Double-check your calculations. Verify the sales tax and ensure that all totals are correct. Computerized cash registers rarely make mistakes.

NORMAL RECEIPT

```
                    0867
CASHIER: Brian F (#130)         Rec: 389
05/17/03  21:35  Swiped      Terminal: 6

                OFFICE DEPOT
                505 Arch Street
                Pittsburgh, PA
                (412) 555-5555
         MERCHANT #: 67985930495955


  CARD TYPE        ACCOUNT NUMBER        EXP
 MASTER CARD     XXXXXXXXXXXX1546        0703

         00 TRANSACTION APPROVED
         AUTHORIZATION #: 544994
          Reference: 04958439339
        TRANS TYPE: Credit Card SALE

 1  staples (box 1000 qty)          $5.44
 4  white bond paper (500ct)       $25.15
 1  Artco pencil sharpener         $12.87
 1  sol. calculator TI1024         $42.42


                    SUBTOTAL:      $85.88
                         TAX:       $6.01
                       TOTAL:      $91.89

         _____

            ***Duplicate Copy***

        Cardholder will pay card issuer above
        amount pursuant to cardholder agreement
```

POORLY MANIPULATED RECEIPT

```
                    0867
CASHIER: Brian F (#130)        Rec: 389
05/17/03  21:35  Swiped        Terminal: 6


                OFFICE DEPOT
                505 Arch Street
                Pittsburgh, PA
                (412) 555-5555
        MERCHANT #: 67985930495955


CARD TYPE        ACCOUNT NUMBER        EXP
MASTER CARD      XXXXXXXXXXXX1546      0703


        00 TRANSACTION APPROVED
        AUTHORIZATION #: 544994
        Reference: 04958439339
        TRANS TYPE: Credit Card SALE


1  staples (box 1000 qty)        $5.44
8  white bond paper (500ct)     $50.30
1  Artco pencil sharpener       $12.87
2  sol. calculator TI1024       $84.84


              SUBTOTAL:   $153.45
                   TAX:     $6.01
                 TOTAL:   $159.46


      _____


          ***Duplicate Copy***

      Cardholder will pay card issuer above
      amount pursuant to cardholder agreement
```

Misaligned type

Incorrect sales tax

Variation in font

OPERATING IN "OFFICE STEALTH MODE"

The less co-workers know about you—without you appearing too secretive or mysterious—and the fewer emotions they have about you, the less gossip there will be (and the fewer embarrassing stories told during the next martini-fueled company party). Ideally, you want to be the "gray man," who is seen but not remembered, liked but not loved, who appears boring rather than fascinating and never shows up for after-work parties.

To be an effective gray man, keep these guidelines in mind:

1   **Never gossip or repeat rumors about others.** Avoid office squabbles where you have to pick sides.

2   **Don't hang around the water cooler, break room, or any other location where gossip takes place.**

3   **Don't dress extravagantly or provocatively.** At long last, it's time to shave that Vandyke and retire the Nehru jacket.

4   **Don't talk or brag about your love life or after-work activities.** Which will be easy if you follow the next suggestion, namely . . .

5   **Don't date any co-workers.** And for that matter . . .

6   **Don't socialize with co-workers after work.** Decline their invitations in a manner that isn't rude. Explain that you have a second job, a

college class each night, a sick mother with gout, or something else that sounds legitimate.

7   **Don't ask probing personal questions about others.** It leaves you vulnerable for the same questions in return.

8   **Always appear polite.** Never voice strong opinions about anything. Never swear or use loud language.

9   **Avoid arguments or discussions about sports, religion, politics, and sex.** People are easily polarized on issues surrounding these topics.

SECURING YOUR COMPANY

Foreign and domestic spies sincerely hope that your company is thriving and prosperous. In fact, they hope your company is so thriving and prosperous that you'll be too damned busy to worry about good security. Here are nine safeguards your competitors hope you haven't utilized yet.

1. **Install an active ID policy that identifies your employees.** Limit the number of entrances to your office to reduce the number of entry points. If your electronic entry system requires a badge or card swipe, add a keypad and require a personal identification number (PIN), too. (The PIN may be the last four digits of each employee's Social Security number or any other assigned number known to the employee, but not to anyone else.) With this additional protection, a lost badge will not allow the finder to enter your offices.

2. **Never allow unannounced visitors to access your facility.** Simply tell them no one is available to escort them, and ask them to schedule an appointment for another date.

3. **Never allow last-minute additions or substitutions to a list of visitors unless there is sufficient time to verify their backgrounds.** Spies thrive on your desire not to inconvenience anyone. An unannounced visitor who has "come so far to see you" is anticipating that your sense of hospitality will override your awareness of good security procedures. Don't fall for this.

4   **Verify personal identification when visitors arrive.** This ensures that visitors are who they say they are. Never accept business cards as identification; always require a passport or other government-issued identification.

5   **Escort all of your guests.** Visitors should never be allowed to wander through your office unescorted. Escorts should be briefed on what is secret or proprietary within the facility and what requires protection.

6   **Educate employees on the difference between "general information" and "company secrets."** Employees should be briefed on the scope of the visit so that they do not discuss unauthorized subjects. Spontaneous technical questions should not be answered unless that information is pre-approved for release.

7   **Ask difficult or disruptive visitors to leave.** If a visitor becomes offended when confronted during a security procedure, be suspicious. Such confrontations are common collection techniques used by spies to assess the level of security at a given company. Ask the visitor to leave immediately.

8   **Treat your office like a rock concert.** Ban cameras, tape recorders, and note-taking.

9   **Keep an eye on the media.** News reporters are essentially spies—never trust reporters with proprietary company information unless you would be comfortable having it disseminated worldwide.

THE MOSCOW RULES

During the Cold War, Moscow was the world's most difficult operating environment for the CIA to conduct secret operations. Innumerable Soviet surveillance specialists kept constant tabs on the CIA officers. To meet with a "source," officers *had* to first lose their surveillance, known as being "in the black" in spy parlance, otherwise they risked compromising the identities of their contacts.

As the cat-and-mouse game of surveillance continued, the CIA developed a series of ad hoc rules that they dubbed the Moscow Rules. These maxims contained the cumulative wisdom of the intelligence officers at the Moscow station inside the U.S. embassy. Here is a selection of the Moscow Rules (compiled by CIA technical officer Tony Mendez) that can be applied to workplaces and corporations of any size:

- **Assume nothing.**
- **Never go against your gut.**
- **Technology will always let you down.**
- **Everyone is potentially under the control of the opposition.**
- **Maintain a natural pace.**
- **Establish a distinctive and dynamic profile and pattern.**
- **Stay consistent over time.**
- **Know the opposition and its terrain intimately.**
- **Build in opportunity but use it sparingly.**
- **Don't harass the opposition.**
- **Pick the time and the place for action.**
- **Any operation can be aborted. If it feels wrong, it's wrong.**

- Keep your options open.
- Use misdirection, illusion, and deception.
- Hide small, operative motions in large, non-threatening motions.
- Float like a butterfly, sting like a bee.
- Once is an accident; twice is a coincidence; three times is an enemy action.
- There is no limit to a human being's ability to rationalize the truth.

SPY PRODUCTS AND SERVICES

If you're anxious to start exploring the activities in this book—and don't have time to comparison-shop—we've found that the following products and services perform exceptionally well.

A2 Copying Restricted Documents

If you're photographing in darkness with a traditional 35 mm camera, we recommend Kodak High-Speed Infrared Film 2481 with Wratten Gelatin Filter 87C. If you want to trade up to a digital model, the high-end Nikon D1 and D100 models are the preferred choices of many professional spies.

A4 Accessing Your Co-workers' Mail

Any cassette-head-cleaner spray containing freon can be used to make envelopes appear translucent. However, as our government continues to limit the use of freon, more and more spies are turning to cans of compressed air. We have had much success with a brand called Kensington Duster II. (Be advised that the manufacturer warns against turning the can upside-down; also be aware that the spray can cause severe burns and/or frostbite to the skin and eyes.)

A8 Covertly Recording Meetings You Attend

Various answering machines will work, but if you're in a hurry, pick up Radio Shack model TAD716 (catalog number 43-716). It uses microcassettes and can record about 45 minutes of conversation.

A9 Covertly Recording Meetings You Cannot Attend

One recommended microcassette recorder is Radio Shack's TeleRecorder model TRC-300 (catalog number 43-476). We've also had success with Radio Shack's omnidirectional Electret Condenser Microphone (catalog number 33-3013).

B5 Safeguarding Your Computer

If you don't want to go through the trouble of generating safe, secure computer passwords, there are machines that will handle the task for you. Mandylion Research Labs sells a Personal Password Manager that stores your passwords and even generates new ones at random. It's small enough to fit on your key chain and costs around $70.

B9 Safeguarding a Meeting

There are plenty of technical security experts who will offer to safeguard your business by sweeping for bugs and other surveillance devices. Unfortunately, many of these people are poorly trained with inadequate equipment. Before you hire anyone, be sure to conduct a thorough background investigation—and ask for references. The following three firms are recognized throughout the United States for their excellent work.

Kevin D. Murray
Murray Associates
P. O. Box 668
Oldwick, NJ 08858-0668
(908) 832-7900

Glenn Whidden
Technical Services Agency
10903 Indian Head Highway
Fort Washington, MD 20744-4018
(301) 292-6430

Richard DiSabatino
Intelligence Support Group Ltd.
7100 Monchae Mountain Boulevard
Inyokern, CA 93527
(323) 650-9193

C7 **Bugging a Trade-Show Event**

Our near-field receiver of choice is the Optoelectronics Xplorer. For price and specs, check out www.optoelectronics.com.

E7 **Transforming a Briefcase into a Bulletproof Shield**

You can buy pretty much anything on the Internet—including body armor. Here are two of our favorite places for one-stop shopping for personal protection gear:

SecurityCosmos.com
http://www.securitycosmos.com

1StopTacticalGear.com
http://www.1stoptacticalgear.com

ACKNOWLEDGMENTS

H. Keith Melton would like to thank Michael Hasco, Vladimir, General Oleg Kalugin, Kevin Murray, Chase Brandon, Tony and Jonna Mendez, Steve Gold, Mick Gould, Dan Mulvenna, Hayden Peake, Gerald "Jerry" Richards, Ralf Beyer and Liane Reinecke, Nigel West, Glenmore Trenear-Harvey, Scott Meinket, Richard DiSabatino, Jim L., Richard Trimbler, David Major and Rusty Capps, Dr. Paul Moore, Toni Hiley, and Sid Boorstein.

Craig Piligian would like to thank his manager, Alan David, for eight years of dedication and hard work; his attorney, Tom Hoberman, for his constant counsel and wise advice; and his executive coordinator, Spencer Rosenberg, for his endless patience and superb organizational skills. Craig is also grateful to all the men and women who have taught him the secrets of tradecraft over the years. Finally, he would like to thank his wife, Lucinda, and his children, Joseph and Amanda, for putting up with all of his strange and mysterious behavior. Without their love and support, his contributions to this book would not have been possible.

Duane Swierczynski would like to thank his wife, Meredith, and his son, Parker. He would also like to thank the illustrator of this book, Stuart Holmes, and all of the good people at Quirk Books and Chronicle Books. And since Duane is convinced that no one ever really reads acknowledgments anyway, he has allowed his publisher to bury the answer to the puzzle in Section B6 right here: There is a deliberate spacing error after the *first* word ("The") on page 48, so you would need to identify the owner of the first binder.

ABOUT THE AUTHORS

H. Keith Melton is a renowned historian and specialist in clandestine devices and equipment. Recognized internationally as an authority on espionage tradecraft, he has amassed an unparalleled collection of spy devices, books, and images of famous spies. Part of his amazing private collection is on permanent display at the Central Intelligence Agency. Keith Melton lectures as a professor at the Counterintelligence Center in Alexandria, Virginia, and is an adviser to U.S. intelligence agencies on historical espionage equipment. He is the author of four highly respected books: *CIA Special Weapons and Equipment, OSS Special Weapons and Equipment, Clandestine Warfare,* and *Ultimate Spy.*

Craig Piligian has been a producer of television programs for the last fifteen years; his work on *Survivor* earned him an Emmy award and two People's Choice awards. For reasons unknown, Mr. Piligian maintains secret classified clearances with the U.S. government.

Duane Swierczynski is a freelance writer living in Philadelphia. His books include *The Perfect Drink for Every Occasion* and *This Here's a Stick-Up!: The Big Bad Book of American Bank Robbery.*